'Milan Kundera wrote that "the struggle of man against power is the struggle of memory against forgetting". In this poignant memoir, Razina Theba serves up the aromatic, bustling Fordsburg of her childhood. At once nostalgic about the simplicity of life and the embrace of family and community, she also sheds light on the double oppression of apartheid and patriarchy as well as the prominent and less visible heroes who stood up to it. In a digital era that incessantly competes for our attention along with the constant threat of revisionist history, this intimate personal story against the backdrop of a grand political milieu reminds us of humanity's ability to continue with the business of living. That life can be full, fun and meaningful even in times of deprivation. And that it is crucial to keep family legacies alive for the next generation.' – Karabo K. Kgoleng

'Forget Zapiro, *Madam & Eve* or the Gupta wedding – Razina Theba's *A Home on Vorster Street* splits your sides, enriches your soul and evokes all the reasons why we love our diversity and who we are.' – Ronnie Kasrils

A home on *Vorster Street*

A Memoir

Razina Theba

Jonathan Ball Publishers
Johannesburg · Cape Town · London

All rights reserved.
No part of this publication may be reproduced or transmitted,
in any form or by any means, without prior permission
from the publisher or copyright holder.

© Text, Razina Theba 2021
© Published edition, 2021 Jonathan Ball Publishers

Originally published in South Africa in 2021 by
JONATHAN BALL PUBLISHERS
A division of Media24 (Pty) Ltd
PO Box 33977
Jeppestown
2043

'Yusuf and Mikaeel', originally published as 'When the father is a better parent', in *Saffron: A Collection of Personal Narratives by Muslim Women*, published in Johannesburg, South Africa by African Perspectives Publishing, 2018.

ISBN 978-1-77619-120-8
eBook ISBN 978-1-77619-121-5

Website: www.jonathanball.co.za
Twitter: www.twitter.com/JonathanBallPub
Facebook: www.facebook.com/JonathanBallPublishers

Cover art by Holmes the Creative
Cover design by Sean Robertson
Author photograph by Saaleha Idrees Bamjee
Design and typesetting by Catherine Coetzer
Set in Utopia

For my parents
Ally and Julie Theba

A note on the language

The use of Gujarati and Arabic in this book is specific to the South African Muslim community of Indian origin that settled in Johannesburg. Any variations of these languages are a result of the evolution of its usage within this context.

Contents

	Prologue	1
1	A Home on Vorster Street	5
2	Right is Right	18
3	The Oriental Plaza	29
4	The Yard	40
5	Favourite Favourite	52
6	What's in a Name?	62
7	Maverick	77
8	Ducking Moose	84
9	Enough is as Good as a Feast	95
10	Julian	107
11	Red Riding Hood	120

12	Christmas Beetles	127
13	Humiliation	141
14	Covert and Overt	157
15	Victims!	167
16	The Wedding	181
17	Yusuf and Mikaeel	188
18	Amaan	193
19	Fig Trees and Restless Geriatrics	211
20	My Dermatologist, the Psychologist	220
	Epilogue	231
	Glossary	235
	Acknowledgements	242

Prologue

Who bears witness to our lives?

My younger son sauntered into our home in Johannesburg's northern suburbs, dropped his school bag on the kitchen floor and asked me, "Mum, when I die, will anybody know that I have lived?"

"Of course! I will know ... Dad will know. If you die when you are older, your kids will know."

It was heavy conversation for a Tuesday afternoon.

"But after how long will everyone who knew me also die – because then nobody will know that I lived."

My child wanted reassurance, not a number. It struck me that with the passage of time, unless one has become famous, this is the cycle of life.

Eventually nobody remembers.

A HOME ON VORSTER STREET

I was born in 1976, into a community trying to create normalcy in an abnormal society stifled by apartheid. I was raised in an area called Fordsburg, located just outside the Johannesburg CBD. It was a mainly Indian suburb. In a tangible expression of separatist state politics, white people generally only visited the area to buy goods at bargain prices from the myriad Indian traders living and working there.

Our world extended for three kilometres in any direction – except on a Friday night, when we would boldly walk down Commissioner Street in the city centre to window-shop and admire the latest fashion at John Orr's. This was a special outing. Financial and physical limitations meant that none of us would feel or wear the clothing. Yet we residents felt a sense of pride in walking through the apartheid bastions.

The history of Fordsburg and the forced removals from nearby Fietas, where many residents had businesses, is well documented.

There is a gap, though.

Who bore witness to the daily lives of the residents of this community?

If personalities are seeds tossed from a basket by God, the mix landed in fertile fields in Fordsburg. Sprouting from this crop were individuals bursting with courage, vibrancy, frustration and a deep understanding of the effects that the politics of the day impacted on their lives.

This memoir is a collection of stories about my extended family, our friends and neighbours, many centred around our home at 33 Vorster Street, Fordsburg.

Prologue

In a world where I battle to compete with technology to hold my son's attention, here is a collection of stories to reassure him that someone, somewhere, always bears witness to our lives.

Chapter 1

A Home on Vorster Street

I learnt a painful lesson about lying when I was six years old. Life was simpler when I was five.

For the first six months of the year, I faked a sore throat every afternoon to avoid attending madressa. I was born into a Muslim home and familiar enough with the rituals of praying five times a day and observing the fast, but the first week of religious schooling put an entirely different spin on my religion. The *apa*, our teacher, spoke to us in idioms. Her favourite line was "Speak the truth, shame the devil".

My tonsils would have still been in my throat had she clarified that idiom and broken it down for us to understand. Like other South Africans, I understood the word "shame" to imply an outpouring of empathy and I had never heard the word in any other context. So I was understandably confused. What I heard were two sentences at odds with each other: "Speak the truth. Shame, the poor devil."

I was not even sure that my parents knew that the *apa* expected me to feel sorry for Satan.

The *apa's* modus for putting the fear of God into our souls was to describe, in painful detail, what would happen to us in the Afterlife if we did not comply with The Rules. It was a baptism of fire. She would remind me to push stubborn strands of my hair into my burka and then stop the class to explain what was going to happen to me in the Afterlife because of my lack of modesty. All I could think of was that my mum, who had lived on earth for many more years than I, did not wear a head covering. I was desperate to get home and warn her about her future in the Afterlife. She was clearly unaware: I would watch her style her short hair with a plug-in hot brush every morning and she would only wear a head covering to funerals. In fact, very few South African Muslim women wore a head covering in the 1980s.

I ran home to our tiny house on Pine Avenue and conveyed this information to my mother. She did not seem overly concerned. Her way of dealing with the news was to tell me, "Allah is forgiving. Don't worry too much about all that."

As she walked past a mirror, she adjusted a wayward curl on her head.

My mother wanted me to attend madressa, nothing would change her mind about that, but she was not about to engage with me on the nuances of getting into Heaven or Hell.

The second week of madressa was Hell. It was my father's turn. The *apa* told us that music is *haram*, forbidden. To

A Home on Vorster Street

drive the point home, she explained that a special section of Hell is reserved for those of us who flaunt that rule. I sat in that classroom feeling guilty as sin when she asked which of us listen to music. By now I knew that lying was my only survival strategy.

Again, I intended to enlighten my parents, but I could hardly get my father's attention over the Hindi tune he was humming. In the evenings our small home would host his friends as they listened to songs by Mohammed Rafi and Kishore Kumar on the LP player. They would argue about which was better while their wives prepared tea and cut slices of sponge cake topped with apricot jam and toasted coconut. My dad was going to Hell for sure.

In fact, my family was going to take up all the special sections in Hell. I felt defeated.

Eventually, I trusted my mother's advice that Allah is forgiving and for months, in the afternoons, would throw myself onto the floor complaining of a sore throat. I thought the game was up when my mum remembered that chronic sore throats in childhood can lead to a weakened heart in adulthood and resolved to have a doctor examine me.

Dr Laher shone his torch down my throat.

"It doesn't look too bad. How often does she suffer?"

Allah is forgiving. Allah is forgiving.

"Really often, Doctor. Sometimes thrice a week. She has been missing so much madressa."

Speak the truth. Shame, the poor devil.

"Shame, the poor thing! I am going to book her in. I think we should pull them out. Does she get a fever with this sore throat?"

"I haven't taken her temperature, but she cries and goes bright red – she can barely speak."

My last performance had been particularly good. I had dug deep.

My tonsils were pulled the following Thursday as a casualty to the *apa's* use of proverbs.

―

Before that fateful Thursday, most days that I had the "tonsillitis attacks" I would be allowed to recover at my maternal grandmother's flat on Vorster Street in Fordsburg. Ma, as I called my grandmother, would help me gargle with salt water and turmeric before settling me into her single bed to wait for my parents to collect me once their business in the Oriental Plaza closed for the day. Often, she would use the afternoon to de-stem bunches of coriander or remove pieces of wood and small stones from packets of lentils.

To do this, she would spread an old tablecloth on her bed and she would work with a tray and some newspaper. Having broken her hip a few years earlier, Ma walked with crutches. The kitchen was a step up from the rest of the flat, so some kitchen chores were undertaken on her bed. The kitchen was also small, with a geyser mounted to the wall, a stove and a four-person kitchen table with stools. No more than three adults could fit into that kitchen and the fridge was kept in her bedroom.

I would lie on Ma's bed while my cousin Shamma prepared her special *slap* chips that I would drench in vinegar, forgetting the nature of the illness I was faking. Sometimes, Khala, Ma's neighbour, would visit and I would watch a

A Home on Vorster Street

Hindi movie with the two elderly women. If nothing else, this "illness" taught me Hindi, a language that nobody in my extended family spoke. My grandparents' roots were in Gujarat province and Bajee and Ma spoke to their children and grandchildren in Gujarati.

My maternal grandfather, Bajee, passed on when I was six but my memories of him are clear. He was a street vendor who sold brown paper shopping bags (recyclable and now fashionably artisanal) from his car which he parked in Diagonal Street in the Johannesburg CBD. For variety, he sometimes sold white Lighthouse candles. His work clothes were a three-piece suit with a pocket watch lodged in his waistcoat and a black fedora hat. His hours of trade were dictated by the setting of the sun and he never missed the *Maghrib* prayers at the Newtown Mosque, which was literally only a few metres away from the flat. Before the *Maghrib* prayer he would come home and expect his cup of chai which would have been brewing for an hour; then he would change into a simple white cotton *kurta* to prepare himself for the prayer. If there was time to spare, he would sit cross-legged on his single bed opposite Ma's bed and recite the Quran.

I recall Bajee being a stern man, dignified and quiet but deeply superstitious. His superstitions had no basis in anything that could be explained. He despised whistling and was easily irritated by loud laughter, believing that we would cry soon after with an intensity proportionate to how heartily we laughed. He would eat food prepared by his daughter Khatija, who was a doctor, but not by Zubeda, who was a nurse. This had more to do with the profession than the daughter.

My cousin Tashmia and I ran past him once as he was trying to concentrate on his recitation of the Quran. He summoned us to stand at his bed and explained patiently that we were being *jungli* – literally, people who inhabit the Indian jungle. Popularly, the word is used to describe uncouth or unruly behaviour, but in my family it was often used to describe my curly hair which could not be tamed. One could be called *jungli* for banging a car door, dishing up more food than one could eat, speaking loudly: the list was endless. The word has acquired an undertone of defiance since it was imported and has now been reappropriated, and collections of cutting-edge jewellery bear the name.

Bajee calmly explained that the best cure when we felt ourselves unable to contain our *jungliness* was to raise our index finger in line with our noses and stare at it to control ourselves. We tried.

An eight-year-old and a five-year-old, like two pressure cookers, pursing our lips together to contain ourselves. It was pointless. Our crossed eyes brought on more laughter and he simply slid his feet into his leather *champals* and left for the mosque. We respected Bajee enough to heed his instruction, but we did not fear him enough to force ourselves to comply.

The best way to describe the Vally family flat on Vorster Street is to picture a nine-block sudoku puzzle. The rooms in the extreme left column opened onto red stoeps, parallel to Vorster Street. From each of these rooms, one could see worshippers walking up the road, past the flat, to the Newtown Mosque. The mosque was close by, at a T-junction at the end of the road. The blocks in the middle column of the sudoku were bedrooms. The rooms in the column on the extreme right (one of which was used as a kitchen) opened into the communal space at the back for all the tenants, with outdoor bathrooms and concrete basins.

This was the Yard.

It was not unusual for tenants living on the first floor to enter the Vally family flat from Vorster Street, greet us and walk right through, exiting the kitchen door to access their flats on the first floor.

It was in this space that Bajee and Ma raised two sons and five daughters. My mother, Julie, was born to my grandparents at a time when boys were more valuable than girls. To this day, bad luck is blamed for the misaligned stars that positioned her as the fifth daughter to be born to a couple desperate for another son.

My grandparents' eldest son, Mohammed Vally, left school at a young age to work and help Bajee support the family. Mohammed's children, grandchildren, nieces and nephews (including me) called him Papa. An extraordinarily gifted cricketer and rugby player, as a boy he would come home with fractured bones and Ma would attend to these by setting his bones with thin planks from tomato boxes. The orthopaedic surgeon who examined the X-ray before Papa's knee replacement surgery in his later years could not believe Ma's handiwork. (There was less marvelling and more horror.)

Accessing decent medical care on Bajee's income was inconceivable so Ma did her best to attend to her children's ailments with her home remedies. Cloves were heated to release their therapeutic oils and ease my mum's painful toothaches. Castor oil was heated and poured into her younger brother Rasid-Ahmed's inflamed ears and countless tomato boxes were dismantled to coax Mohammed's broken bones into setting. Ma treated chesty coughs by sewing a red flannel vest to wear against the skin to warm the chest and clear the lungs. My mum's sister Hajira passed on at 50, having suffered numerous untreated strep throat infections, which led to rheumatic heart disease. This condition arose from the cramped and damp conditions she lived in as a child, in Vorster Street. Ma's salt water and turmeric concoction was no match for the bacterial infection.

These are the nuances of poverty. Every one of my mum's siblings carried into adulthood these ailments, which would have been easily remedied by a consultation with a doctor in their childhood. My grandparents had not attended school. That they raised seven children, six of whom matriculated, with two of them becoming doctors, one a nurse and another a teacher, in the 1960s, is nothing short of remarkable. Papa left school to help his father support his siblings but his general knowledge, emotional intelligence and love of reading were unparalleled. He read every newspaper every day and one of his last phone calls to me before his cancer diagnosis was to recommend that I buy the *Sunday Times* newspaper just to read Ndumiso Ngcobo's column: "That man has the funniest stories."

Papa married my aunt Amina, whom my sibling and I called Gorimummy. As was customary in many Indian households, they and their children lived with Bajee and Ma. At this stage my mum's eldest sister had married and

A Home on Vorster Street

relocated to Lichtenburg in what is now the North West Province. *Her* four children, my cousins, were sent to live on Vorster Street to attend high school as those in her area did not admit Indians. At its most crowded, the flat housed Bajee, Ma, Papa and Gorimummy, their children, the four remaining sisters and those four cousins.

The standard meal was *kari-kitchri* made from bimri rice (never basmati, which was more expensive) and flavoured sour milk without the accompanying side dishes of fried potatoes, spinach and pumpkin. Salads were prepared as a treat for special occasions. Years ago, if one wanted to indicate to a guest that she had overstayed her welcome, the host would serve *kari-kitchri*. It was regarded as rather a poor substitute for a meal, but with Bajee as the sole breadwinner, and before his children could contribute to the bills, this was standard fare. Strangely, the stigma attached to *kari-kitchri* has disappeared over time. It is now served at glamorous weddings with at least seven accompanying dishes.

After returning from Cape Town, where he had been studying, my younger uncle, Rasid-Ahmed, and his family lived on Vorster Street while he completed his internship at Baragwanath Hospital. Fortunately, by then most of his sisters had married and moved out. One night, he returned from his shift ridiculously late at night and he and his wife Anisa had an argument about the obviously unequal distribution of child-rearing duty. That she agreed to share this flat with his parents and 13 other people, with a room located at the dead centre of the sudoku block, while pregnant, nursing an older child who had come down with the flu and using an outdoor communal toilet – while he worked a 12-hour shift doing what he *loved* – is a miracle.

In Ma's version Rasid-Ahmed was apologising profusely and in my Aunty Anisa's version he was giving as good as he was getting. Both women agree that Anisa lifted a bottle of cough syrup, took aim and launched it at her target. Luckily, the absorbent floral wallpaper took the worst of it and Ma and Bajee, who were there, ducked to avoid being hit. Aunty Anisa threw that bottle, ignoring the fact that Rasid-Ahmed was their laatlammetjie, male and a doctor and she was a daughter-*in*-*law* in a traditional Indian home. She was fabulous.

—

By the time I was duping my mother with fake sore throats the resident list of the home on Vorster Street had changed. Bajee had passed on but Papa and his family continued to live with Ma. All my mum's sisters had married and moved out and my cousins and I became the third-generation "residents" of the flat. Apart from Papa's family and Ma, we actually all lived elsewhere but we converged at every opportunity. Papa encouraged every action that Bajee would have dismissed as *jungli* behaviour from his nieces and nephews.

The Saturday ritual I was born into was afternoon tea at Ma's house. As the new head of the family, Papa would buy crispy brown rolls and koeksisters from Mono Bakery and Gorimummy would spread margarine and prepare tea while we all crammed into Ma's bedroom to watch local soccer, or another of Papa's favourites, boxing. He sat on a

A Home on Vorster Street

particular bench wedged between two single beds and he would lean against the wall. Next to him would be a 30-pack of Peter Stuyvesant cigarettes. He would make abrupt moves as though he were in the ring himself. Watching Papa watch a boxing match was joyful entertainment.

The Rothmans July Handicap, the most glamorous horse racing and camp fashion event, prompted high excitement for my cousins and me. Papa came up with the idea that we should form a kitty (for which he would provide the cash) and we each picked the number of a horse from a bowl. It felt like such a wholesome family ritual but I wonder what the men who walked along the road to the Newtown Mosque would have thought if they knew that the door to the flat on Vorster Street was closed – for only that one day a year – to facilitate organised gambling.

Papa gave each of his nieces his undivided attention, calling us his darlings. After his passing each of us had the unshakeable belief that we had been his favourite.

The tenants of the Yard were a mixture of Hindus, Muslims, Christians and Farsis, but we identified strongly with each other as being second and third generation immigrants. We celebrated Diwali along with the Hindu children, wearing our *punjabis* and marvelling at the little lights that were lit in the week up to the celebration. On Diwali, all the Hindu neighbours would send a plate of sweetmeats to their Muslim neighbours and vice versa for Eid. My cousins and I would be sent out in groups to deliver Eid plates filled with sweetmeats, biscuits and tarts.

Our sweetmeats were never as good as the ones the Hindu women made, and Ma and her daughter-in-law

Gorimummy would console themselves by sending an extra plate of *bajias*, a deep-fried fritter, to compensate for our shortcomings. Ma made the best *bajias* in the Yard. Often, as we were about leave the flat on delivery, we would be called back and Ma would throw a few more *bajias* into an already overflowing plate. How many *bajias* each family received from us was proportionate to how well Ma's milky *barfee* set. Perfect *barfee* meant a dozen *bajias* and sticky soft *barfee* that did not set and stuck to the lunch wrap warranted two dozen *bajias*.

Before the sunset prayer, an adult would shout at us, "Get into the house, it's *Maghrib* time," just as the smell of frying onions hung thick in the air. Men would close the bonnets of their unreliable cars and give up on trying to buff scratches off. The residents of the Yard would settle down for the evening.

—

My cousins and I are now parents. We schedule get-togethers months in advance and drag our children with us so that they can meet their cousins. There is no Ma's house to converge on and no Yard for our children to play in. Our children stand around awkwardly and nod politely while we share our memories. Mostly, they are distracted by their mobile devices and pay little attention. One of us will always bring koeksisters. We wonder what has happened to some of the people that we knew as children. We understand each other's idiosyncrasies intimately and avoid looking at our children as they try to stare us down, wanting to leave.

Some things do hit home, though.

Going home recently, my children jumped into the car and Mikaeel said, "You would LIE for a whole SIX months to avoid going to madressa? Geez, Mum!"

And for the first time in my life, I felt as though my son believed that I, too, was a child once.

Chapter 2

Right is Right

For my friend Cassim Boorany, who loved this story.
24 April 1961–23 January 2021

Most people I know have a characteristic expression that they use no matter what the situation is. I tend to mumble the words "true-true-true" in response to incidents that are conveyed to me. It does not necessarily mean that I agree, but it is my contribution to confirm that I am listening when I'm bored and I sometimes use it to propel the story along.

My dad's characteristic expression is "right-is-right". It is used to describe the absurdity of paying for a beverage at a coffee shop when one's grocery cupboard has coffee in stock. This is the world-view of the generation that would not attend a wedding unless the hosting family took the

Right is Right

time to visit with a personal invitation as well as a card to confirm the finer details. It took him a week to wrap his head around the idea that a gift registry might be added to the card the first time he encountered that, asking me, "So this tells me what gift I must buy?" He is mortified by the idea of a "bring and braai", adamant that the person whose idea the braai was should foot the bill, well, because "right-is-right".

So, when the family was invited personally to my cousin's wedding in Maputo in the mid 1980s, my father graciously accepted the invitation. His brother, my paternal uncle, visited us in Pine Avenue on a Sunday afternoon after confirming that we would be home. He drank chai, ate samoosas, chatted about inconsequential events and left a printed invitation in Portuguese detailing the exact address in Maputo with a map and directions to the venue.

"That is how you invite!" My father beamed, because "right-is-right".

Before my uncle left, he pored over the invitation with my father. Neither of them spoke a word of Portuguese but the honour and significance of the official document warranted an attempt at translating the card.

Mozambique was drenched in a bloody civil war. There were reports of mass killings, rape and torture and there was seemingly no safe passage to follow the directions on the invitation and attend the wedding. Initially my mother thought that the invitation was hilarious. She said it was as good as "being invited to the moon". As days passed though, it became apparent to us all that my dad was determined to attend because "right-is-right". He would not dishonour his brother with his absence by using the feeble excuse that the venue was in the heart of a war zone. Besides, he had directions and a personal invitation. Nothing would stop him.

My father and his five brothers met to work out the logistics of transporting 75 members of the Theba clan to Maputo in one piece while their wives conspired, in vain, to avoid the wedding altogether. Suddenly, my mum's interest in the civil war escalated and she took to gathering as much intelligence as was possible at the time. What started as an ode of devotion to "right-is-right" was spiralling out of control, and the inevitability of spending Christmas in Maputo was dawning on my mother. Once she realised there was no going back, she bequeathed all her gold jewellery to her sisters in anticipation of her death as a civilian casualty of war.

The plan was as follows:

All the nuclear families would leave Johannesburg, Lenasia and Laudium at carefully staggered departure times to meet at Komatipoort at 5am on Christmas morning. Cars would be housed by a farmer in Komatipoort, in exchange for a pot of biryani, twelve dozen samoosas and some spares for his Hilux bakkie.

We would all board a train from Komatipoort to Ressano Garcia (which the South African relatives lazily called Rosana Gracia), where we would switch trains.

This was the part my father was most proud of. He and his brothers had somehow hired a luxury train that had belonged to Samora Machel, the president of Mozambique, in order to transport the family safely into the heart of Maputo. The Blue Train, by the sound of things, had nothing on the presidential carriage. Bullet-proof three-inch-thick

Right is Right

windows, an air conditioner, a plush leather interior and an in-house chef would accompany us to Maputo.

My dad and my mum had embarked on a silent war, choosing to talk through my sister and me. He would say things like, "Well if it's good enough to transport the President of a country, I think that your mother will be comfortable enough." Mostly, when speaking to me he would refer to her as "your mum", but this month she was "your mother". Too young to appreciate the pomp and ceremony, we would nod wide-eyed and eager. I often wonder why my mum simply didn't refuse to go. But I guess it would have been doing a disservice to her fatalistic personality. Besides, her funeral arrangements had been carefully communicated to her family and served as an example of my father's unreasonableness, the retelling of which could have bankrupted the family since Telkom weren't offering the R300 flat rate yet. She considered herself a martyr to the mantra of "right-is-right".

After midnight on Christmas Eve we left for Komatipoort, my sister and I cocooned in the back of our white Datsun, my dad humming his favourite tunes. My mum shoved an ice-cream tub overflowing with egg bread into my father's hands. "The Last Supper" she called it, not missing an opportunity to confirm her sainthood.

In Komatipoort, a final headcount was taken, egg bread from Lenz to Laudium was passed around and flasks of chai were downed by my father and his brothers, who were all in a congratulatory mood after the first leg of the journey. As the sun rose, we started the charming train ride to Ressano Garcia. The earlier humming gave way to full-on belting out of the Hindi tunes as the six brothers went on their way to honour their eldest brother by attending his son's wedding.

What could possibly go wrong?

Samora Machel's train. The brothers stood on the platform with their mouths agape, barely able to make eye contact with their wives. The carriages that sat on the tracks were bullet-riddled, rusted and dilapidated. The putrid smell of raw sewage from the train kept the clan firmly on the platform, with my mother gagging involuntarily when the wind blew in her direction. Seventy-five people in the family and the only sound was a bird called Piet calling to his wife. The Theba men were avoiding theirs, hoping that somehow, somehow, the pile of rubbish in front of them would morph into a luxurious carriage.

It must have been three minutes later that a volley of bullets and exploding grenades nearby silenced the Piet-my-vrou and sent everyone charging towards the train. It was a rude reminder to us that we were on the outskirts of a civil war. Arms and limbs and heads banged against each other as the train set off for Maputo.

As my uncle tried to count heads in the mishmash of confusion, my mother wryly remarked that we were all fortunate that it wasn't a body count.

Only once the basics, like the fact that we were all indeed alive, had been taken care of did the conditions in the train hit us. What might have been a maroon leather interior was torn, as if massacred by machetes, exposing the foam stuffing which had burst out in freedom. The foam was coated in mould and mildew and the train smelt as if it had been

Right is Right

used to transport rotting carcasses. And there was another stench. All 75 of us Thebas moved to the furthest end of the train, barely able to breathe. We had not inspected the toilets but had a sure idea of where they were located.

The very young children simply cried, as small children do, and one of the wives told her husband to open the windows. Which man would be brave enough to break the news that the windows were welded shut?

"It's 88 kilometres, three hours maximum," my father announced, as my mum retrieved a scarf from her bag to wipe down her forehead and breathe through as a shield. Her sister-in-law, my *motima*, was cheerfully making a number of calculations on a piece of paper, oblivious to the smell, the heat and the chaos.

"*To hoo kareh*, what are you doing?" my mum asked through the silk scarf, peering over at the piece of paper.

"Splitting the community of property," she replied. My mother was convinced that she had taken her malaria tablets later than the rest of us. She looked positively cheerful.

If there was any chance that her marriage would be saved after this trip, it dissipated when the train stopped abruptly 15 minutes into the journey. The train driver simply did not know how to operate a train, nor did he have a schedule of the other trains that would be sharing the line. His predecessor had returned to Portugal after Mozambique's independence in 1975 and taken the instruction manual and schedule with him, in a malicious show of spite. He thought it best to stop the train every eight kilometres or so for half an hour at a time to avoid a head-on collision with another train.

Of course, this is the synopsis of a conversation which took an hour, in different languages.

Afonso, the driver, could easily have been relaying a Mozambican fable or love story. The men tossed a coin to see which of them would speak to the women about this recent development.

My dad stood at the head of the train, clasped his hands together reverently and cleared his throat dramatically with the enthusiasm of a Sunday preacher.

"Well, Afonso is slowing down the train and allowing us to take in the scenery of a free, liberated Mozambique!" It was the best he could do. We looked out at the dry bushveld through mud-splattered windows and when we turned back, my dad had disappeared to the front of the train. The putrid smell had nothing on my mother's gaze.

The journey took 12 hours and Afonso relieved the Theba brothers of their watches, one by one, at every stop to get us into Maputo before nightfall. Severely dehydrated and damp, we limped up the stairs to our rooms in the Polana Hotel. For some reason the receptionist thought it best not to mention that water restrictions were in place until 6am the following morning.

We looked as though we had lived through the war. Some wives used the strength they had left to quarrel with their husbands loudly and with abandon, while the strategic thinkers thought it best to conserve energy and replace lost fluid before the onslaught.

"It's alright, we are here now." The conviction of "right-is-right" had morphed into "it will be alright". I could tell my dad didn't believe a word he said.

Right is Right

The fumigation of our room at the Polana Hotel was not his fault at all. Of all the things to do in a hotel room, spraying toxic amounts of Doom would not be high on anyone's list – except my mother's. One can hardly call it a phobia; it is not at all an irrational aversion. In this case, it was an ant in the sugar bowl that brought on her obsession to hunt down any members of the insect kingdom that may have been lurking. She's a bad-ass like that.

Within minutes, thousands of cockroaches, centipedes and spiders emerged, writhing from the assault to their central nervous systems. She stood rooted to the spot for a few seconds before drawing her green weapon and trying to spot-treat the problem. By now, they were pouring out from the ceilings, wardrobes and under the carpet, some falling off the ceiling onto my sleeping sister and me. She depressed the aerosol button and didn't stop until the can coughed up its last drops. By then, the fumes had disturbed nests that weren't in the initial line of fire and these insects were spinning furiously and moving spasmodically but not dying.

Abandoning my sister and me, Mum ran down the hallway screaming hysterically. My dad and his brothers, who had retreated to a cigar room to play bridge and commiserate about their miserable wives, ran past her towards our room. Fully expecting to confront a rebel soldier, they charged into the room and grabbed my sister and me, carrying us into the hallway.

This incident levelled the playing fields between my parents, my dad believing that his misdirected optimism in planning the holiday had been vindicated by my mother's stupidity.

A HOME ON VORSTER STREET

—

The beach wedding was beautiful and we were received graciously by the hosts. The brothers were elated to reunite with their sisters, two of whom had married Mozambican men decades previously. By contrast the children of my *fois* – my father's sisters – regarded us with some ambivalence and, at times, casual disregard. In hindsight, we were like those wealthy cousins from a developed country who spook easily and complain endlessly. Communication was limited to them bringing their five fingers together and lifting them to their mouths to ask if we had eaten and us giving them a thumbs-up signal followed by bringing the index finger and thumb together to indicate that the food was excellent. My mother and I don't eat prawns, but everyone else in our entourage did.

Eat prawns? If ever there was a euphemism. My aunts drowned their sorrows in the buttery garlicky speciality and one could almost hear them thinking that the one redeeming feature of this holiday would be eating copious amounts of prawns cooked to perfection. They started modestly, telling each other, "I'm not a big eater, you go ahead," but the evidence kept piling up until the shells were spilling out of the containers that had been thoughtfully placed between the women. They kept coming, platters and platters of prawns, freshly prepared. Knowing that my mum and I don't eat prawns, a peri-peri chicken was considerately placed between us just at the tail end of my dad telling his sisters how he would not have missed this function for the world because, one thing, "right-is-right".

Right is Right

A cool sea breeze, a brand-new marriage and me dozing off on my father's lap. Had the experience ended on this note, my dad would have had bragging rights forever. My mother was touched by being the recipient of the only chicken at the wedding, and still smarting from the Doom incident, so she nodded her approval when my dad suggested that all the kids play in the warm beach sand. Ordinarily, she would have flatly refused; night swimming would not be something she would consider safe. But this was arguably the most beautiful beach in the world and we would be leaving for home the next day.

Within seconds, all six Theba brothers were fishing children out of the bluebottle-infested water lapping the sand and pouring vinegar on our legs. Our Mozambican relatives desperately tried to feign concern but were ultimately peeved at the South African part of the family, which attracted catastrophe like pollen would a bee. We were not unlike the tourists who stick their heads out of cars at the Kruger Park to take selfies with lions.

One up for my mother. Her sour mood returned and she was looking forward to going home. There was no avoiding Samora Machel's train again; only now, the family had secured the real McCoy. It turned out that a corrupt official had pocketed the initial payment and sent us an abandoned train for the journey to Maputo. The family paid twice as much to secure the real thing for our journey home.

So considerate were my Mozambican relatives that they sent tons of prawns to the Hotel Polana to be served to the party before we departed. We only left once the last one was eaten.

The new train was marginally better. Windows still welded, no aircon, but the seats were decent and there was no stench. And then it started, with my middle *motima*. For the third time on this trip, her marriage looked precarious. She jumped up suddenly and took off towards the toilet, taking a *jajroo* (toilet) bottle with her. She returned looking ashen. Within the hour, 73 members of the clan had food poisoning. The kids were vomiting, abandoned by their mums, who were waiting desperately to use a toilet whose flushing mechanism had given up 20 kilometres ago. Shoes were thrown out of packets and used to catch the remains. Men were crawling to the toilet. My mother grabbed my hand and led me to the open door of the train, where the breeze offered some reprieve from the widespread gastro.

For a second, I thought she was going to jump, but then, with a small smile playing on her lips, she sat down next to me, both our feet dangling out of the train. She smiled at me. "We really should get out of their way, right-is-right."

Chapter 3

The Oriental Plaza

It was a chilly winter's day in Fordsburg when Lady Di got married. I was five years old and I distinctly remember the day being in Ramadan. My mum was baking biscuits for Eid and she kept bringing me the imperfect ones to eat and moving between kitchen and lounge to get glimpses of the day unfolding on TV. My mum hates wastage, but the biscuits kept burning when she lingered too long at the TV offering a stream of criticism, and so plates of coconut biscuits kept coming my way. The tiny home I shared with my parents and sister smelt of a mixture of vanilla and coal from the anthracite stove. It was no coincidence that she chose this day to take the morning off work and bake. My mum had a vested interest in the wedding day because it was an opportunity to voice her opinion about the royal wedding gown.

Before I was born in 1976, my mum ran three dressmaking schools, in Fordsburg, Fietas and Jeppe Street in the Johannesburg CBD. Here, she taught mostly Indian women how to cut, pin and sew in the Italian style of dressmaking. A perfectionist, her training and subsequent style were inspired by tailored dresses that hugged the body like a glove. Lady Di's wedding gown was, in her opinion, an ill-fitting explosion of creased ivory silk with enormous puffy sleeves that swallowed up her petite frame. And that untidy bow – an embarrassment to dressmakers everywhere. She took it personally and kept offering me variations on what she would have done, had she been commissioned to design the gown. I was altogether more impressed with eating biscuits for lunch. Her sisters and sisters-in-law placed a high premium on what Julie thought of the wedding gown and the phone rang all day.

"Can somebody please straighten that crooked bow!" My mum was the expert and on this day, as she has right through my life, she offered her opinion decisively.

If I am forced to draw an analogy, 39 years later, it would be my explanation of *dolus eventualis* in the Oscar Pistorius murder trial. *It is when you do something criminal knowing that it is criminal and then you say that you did not know it was criminal.* This insignificant section in criminal law was taught to us about three-quarters through a lecture, for ten minutes, and there were no questions from students. Lay people do not know that an attorney's work is often administrative, mundane and dispassionate so this was our opportunity to shine. Almost every attorney who did not practise criminal law had to google these Latin words again.

The Oriental Plaza

That my inner circle of friends *valued* what I thought of the judge's decision in this trial gave me the feeling that my mum must have had on that wintery day in Fordsburg. I was young but it was a reminder to me that my mum came with a history of her own.

She closed her dressmaking schools when she was pregnant with me, something that may explain why almost any white noise makes me drowsy. The whirr of the Singer sewing machines was the first sound I ever heard.

The plan was to have my hair cut at Crazy-Old-Stix hair salon later that afternoon in preparation for Eid. This, after the disappointing balcony kiss at Buckingham Palace. *Bad gown, bad kiss, these people waste my time!* By now, my mum was annoyed with British dressmakers and she needed to run several errands before returning to our shop in the Oriental Plaza. Unlike my father, who can hold a grudge forever and a day, during the ten-minute walk past the Oriental Plaza, up Avenue Road and into Central Road, my mum found it in herself to forgive the princess. She burst into the hair salon and announced, "Let's do something different from a Purdey. Give her a Lady Di."

The Purdey haircut is an androgynous *skottel* cut that I was convinced was the only style Aunty Florence was trained in. She sucked on her Courtleigh cigarette with one hand and flipped my hair from one side of my face to the other, hoping that a path would reveal itself, while getting a feel for the texture of my hair. To turn my dark mop of thick curls into a Lady Di was going to be impossible.

It turned out for the best that the royal wedding was on a Wednesday. Saturdays always drew a large contingent of shoppers to the Oriental Plaza, so our shop would have been busy and my dad would have insisted that she read about the wedding in *The Star* newspaper's late edition, which was hand-delivered to the shop daily.

The Oriental Plaza, a vast shopping mall in Fordsburg housing 360 traders, was built in the 1970s. As part of apartheid spatial planning, traders who had established businesses in 14th Street, Fietas, were forced to move to the Oriental Plaza and rent shops at exorbitant rentals. The ultimate purpose of this planning project was to turn Fietas into a whites-only area.

Entering into negotiations to get the buy-in of the traders, who ran successful businesses, would have given them a false sense that they had a say, so they were quite literally bulldozed into trading at the Oriental Plaza. This did not happen in one fell swoop, as the Oriental Plaza was built in sections, with the North Mall renting out space to traders first. The Soweto Uprisings in 1976 halted the relocation but by then, enough businesses and homes had been bulldozed to make trading in Fietas no longer viable. People of Indian heritage the world over are known for their tenacity, resilience and entrepreneurial spirit, and the traders took on the challenge of making their businesses in the Oriental Plaza successful with grudging determination.

In this way, the jazzy, soulful vibe that only a mixture of Malays, Indians, Chinese, Coloureds, Africans, Jews, Lebanese and Afrikaners living in close proximity together could create was replaced by a themed shopping experience, packaged inside a modernist shopping centre that spanned fifteen city blocks. A rather patronising nod to the Orient

The Oriental Plaza

was evident in the souk-like marketplace set-up devised by the architects. The gold-coloured brick in the courtyards of the North and South Mall sections and their open air kiosks, as well as the octagon inlays of the arcade ceilings, all worked towards the theme. The Grand Bazaar, a three-storey circular section, was lit by gigantic wrought-iron globe structures covered in ruby-coloured cloth, suspended dramatically from the ceiling with industrial-strength chains. The Peacock Fountain, a steel bird with fanned-out feathers and water shooting out of pipes, sat in the courtyard of the North Mall, where a clock tower adorned with minarets was erected to orientate customers by serving as a landmark. This minaret lines up almost exactly with the Newtown Mosque minaret on Vorster Street.

White customers would purchase samoosas made for mass consumption and sit on the edge of the Peacock Fountain eating their *driehoek koelie-koek*. Some of them would ask for samoosas by this name, which perhaps explains why traders sold gigantic, oily samoosas with thick doughy *pur* which had bubbled from being unlovingly dunked into too-hot oil. No self-respecting Indian would consume that heavy triangle masquerading as a samoosa in their own home. I suspect that the green bullet chillies were not sliced very finely either.

Karma has a name. It was a samoosa purchased at the Oriental Plaza in the 1980s.

My parents and Papa rented Shop 242 in the South Mall. Most traders who moved to the Oriental Plaza from Fietas were general dealers, which meant that a single shop could sell cutlery, bridal fabric and dashboard cleaner. This was part of what made shopping in the hustle and bustle so much fun: one never knew what one might find. By contrast, the developers of the Plaza attached strict conditions to what could be sold in each business. My parents had to introduce a unique line of goods so as not to compete with merchants who were old hands at the trading game.

And so, before flea markets and craft markets, my folks started one of only two curio shops in the greater Johannesburg area. The other one was in the Carlton Centre. My parents depleted their creative juices coming up with the idea of a curio shop and then named it "Mystic Curios". Using their surname, Theba, would have been more appropriate – it was an obvious choice that would have lent some quasi-authenticity to the products on offer. They sold wooden African masks, soapstone busts of African men and women, carved wooden elephants, cheetahs, rhinos and almost everything touristy one could think of. For Show and Tell in Grade 1 I took a glass paper weight with grassy mud and a giant orange sticker which said "100% Pure South African Elephant Shit".

Zulu love letters were a fast seller, as they were the perfect small token to hand out to colleagues and they were light enough to pack without exceeding the baggage allowance. These gorgeous colourful "letters" were made up of different patterns of colours with each colour chosen to convey a particular meaning. In the early 1980s, every American tourist who visited the Oriental Plaza returned home from their safari in Africa with piles of Zulu love letters. Unbeknown to them, some of them proposed marriage to their bosses.

The Oriental Plaza

Large copper plaques with 3D animals against a black painted bushveld setting would render tourists indecisive. They desperately wanted to take these home, but they were bulky and heavy. In a last-ditch attempt to clinch the sale my dad would say, "Phone me from the airport and I will collect it from you and refund your money if it doesn't fit in your luggage." In twenty odd years, we never received a call from Jan Smuts airport so either those gaudy plaques are adorning homes the world over or there are several hundred of them in an airport storage room.

The price marked on an item was never the price that shoppers were expected to pay and traders enjoyed haggling with shoppers. My dad's line to shoppers when he was asked for a discount was "You are killing me!" but when he was not asked for a better price, he would offer to "work something out" for them. He would fake-crunch the numbers on a calculator, his profit being quite secure, and then show the customer the screen on the calculator and gesture towards me and say, "My children must also eat."

Raising a child in a shopping centre is not ideal, but when I was not being a sales prop I busied myself playing the African musical instruments. For fun I would sometimes wear an African mask and walk around the shop nonchalantly when customers walked in, until my mum realised how unsettling this was for customers and she made me promise to stop. On days when my marimba-playing skills grated their nerves, I would take a walk around the Oriental Plaza and visit other shopkeepers.

In the early days of the Oriental Plaza, very few shoppers frequented the new centre. Traders had time on their hands and I would visit and chat. Some traders would regale me with stories about the heyday of Fietas and confide how much they despised living in the dustbowl of Lenasia. I would listen attentively, drinking in all the information. I presume that they were reassured that their stories were being passed on to a younger generation. As I left, they would give me a small item from their shops. The owner of Discount Cycle and Toys would give me chalk and I called him Chalk-Uncle. The uncle from Everyman's Luck would give me a tiny ornament to fill my printer's tray. The aunty from the candy store would give me a Chappies. She was Chappies-Auntie. Sometimes my mum would make me return some of the items, but the traders always insisted that I keep them. It is a cultural thing to send a guest off with a small token for having taken the time to visit. In exchange, and I balk at this memory, I would sing a song for them. For a reason that is probably equally embarrassing, I knew every word of Boney M's "By the Rivers of Babylon" and would belt this song out on request. There is a beautiful age between three and six when precocious children are not yet self-conscious, and it was in these years of my childhood, before school, that the traders in the Oriental Plaza *were* my family.

In the Grand Bazaar an old man would don a Father Christmas outfit every December and pose for photos with children against a wooden backdrop covered in crinkly foil and polystyrene snow. He would sit in a white sleigh made from chipboard and his old tape recorder would play "Jingle Bells" on Side A and B. He was really a genuinely old man with watery blue eyes, red tear troughs, dark brown age

The Oriental Plaza

spots and broken capillaries on his face. He and I became friends and he would gift me a photo of the two us every year at no charge. Our friendship started under strange circumstances. Being an inquisitive but bored three-year-old, I would sit on a step for hours snacking on peanuts or candyfloss watching children pose for pictures with Father Christmas. Children of colour would stand next to him awkwardly, as if they were being called to attention, while the white children would jump onto his lap and smile confidently at the photographer. He noticed me sitting there, left his post and took the lift to the third floor to management's office to report the abandoned child. He was in my line of vision until I watched him disappear into the offices. It was unusual to see him move; he usually just took a short break shuffling towards the toilets but never left his little studio. He came down several minutes later with the manager and gestured towards me.

"That little girl! She's Mystic's daughter from the South Mall! No, I wouldn't worry about her. She knows this centre like the back of her hand. She's a Plaza baby."

The section of the Oriental Plaza where my parents' shop was located was the runt of the centre. It leased shops to tenants who had been slow on the draw in committing to rent. A controversy impossible to ignore was that some families who led the charge against the apartheid government relocating traders to the Oriental Plaza were the very same families who had secured prime positions for themselves in the North Mall. With the Peacock Fountain, the clock tower and the Grand Bazaar having devoured the budget, the South Mall by contrast had no mass appeal. To add insult to injury, the South Mall was built on Freedom Square, which was an open community square that saw the launch of the Defiance Campaign in 1952. Parts of Freedom Square were used as a car park and the remainder was absorbed into the Oriental Plaza. Until a heritage plaque was erected, there was nothing to mark the historical, social and cultural significance of this spot.

Across the walkway directly outside our shop were vendors in little kiosks selling smaller items like incense sticks, fruit and vegetables, miniature Hindu deities and china fruit. Setting up their wares every morning took hours. I felt sorry for these traders, as afternoon summer showers would drive customers into the shops in the arcades, while they covered their goods with sails and waited, sometimes in vain, for the weather to clear. My mother's rule was that if it started raining, I was to return to our shop immediately as the aisles would get busy with customers. I would sit near the doorway of our shop and watch the vendors wipe all their items dry and pack them into boxes in the hope that the next day would be a better trading opportunity. For these traders, with such uncertain trading opportunities, the loss of being forced out of Fietas would have been impossible to quantify.

―

Forty years later, I visit the Oriental Plaza about once a month. Many shops, including our shop, are now rented to immigrants but there remain some of the original tenants, now owners, whose children and grandchildren opted to continue the family business. If the original owners are

The Oriental Plaza

there, by now quite elderly, with failing sight and hearing, I am often told how much I look like my mother and they still call me "Mystic's daughter". I step on my husband's toes gently when he offers to pay the marked price on an item. This is family, I tell him. I will get a discount.

Chapter 4

The Yard

It would have been easy to miss the entrance to the Yard. On a narrow side road, just off the bustle of Bree Street, was an opening between two double-storey buildings. A short driveway opened into a massive courtyard with flats in a U-shape, the homes on Vorster Street making up one side of the U. The word "driveway" evokes images of suburbia, but I am being generous. My parents, aunts and uncles would drive up at a slight incline and then struggle with the car in first gear until the driveway was navigated. It was rocky, the concrete cracked and broken. Dangerous slabs threatened to erupt and penetrate the undercarriage. The width demanded that they drive at a snail's pace, causing the least interference to the jigsaw assortment of concrete. About halfway through and a third of the way across was a giant pothole. Residents took turns filling it with sand, cardboard, bricks and newspapers but the "repair" would last a day or two and eventually spill all the well-meaning intentions onto the already uneven road.

A characteristic of the residents of the Yard, apart from us all being of Indian origin and sharing outdoor toilets, was that all the adults drove cars that were scraped on the front left corner. What was left after avoiding the pothole would barely allow a vehicle through. The drivers' expressions were always the same. A deep breath as they switched to second gear and then paused to compose themselves. Passengers fell silent, heart rate increasing, because this manoeuvre required concentration. Radios would be turned down. No matter how tall the driver was, they would lift their head and keep an eye on the front left corner of the car, lips pursed. When you all felt the inevitable scrape, faces would contort in a physical reflection of the pain the car must have felt. Passengers and the driver would disembark and everyone would examine the damage.

Welcome to the Yard.

To the immediate left were rows of communal toilets with wooden doors whose panels had started to rot and break off. I would stare at the rows of closed doors and decide which one offered the most privacy. Ankles were inevitably exposed and the toilets were gender neutral. Most children stopped all intake of liquid after 6pm, a subtle inconvenience resulting from having a toilet outside of the flat. One's best bet, if desperate, was to bargain and negotiate with an older sibling or cousin to accompany you and keep *aara* (a lookout) outside the toilet door. Of course, one could be double-crossed and just as you sat down to relieve yourself, the saviour you had secured would turn into an evil persecutor and bang furiously on the toilet door to remind you never to ask them again. Naturally, they would feign innocence when you emerged ashen-faced and shaking with fear.

Parking was never allocated but it made sense to park directly outside one's flat. Guests would line up neatly behind the family's car, still smarting from the raw scrape to their car. The communal space was a gigantic opening of gravel and small pebbles which made a crunching noise as cars parked for the night.

The flats in the U-shaped commune were little cells in the honeycomb of the Yard, housing extended families cocooned into little enclaves on the property.

It was grey and dreary except for one thing: a massive jasmine creeper outside Ma's flat. I have never seen a plant flourish with such minimal care. After a hot sticky day, an afternoon Highveld thunderstorm would carry the scent of jasmine into Ma's flat. Some families have a theme song, others have a specific signature dish, and the Vally family still venerates the smell of jasmine. Just last week, my cousin Anisa sent a picture to the family WhatsApp group of herself, nose a bright red, flecks of snow sticking to her hair and her tiny face peeping out of a winter hoodie, holding a jasmine seedling at a nursery in New York with the caption, "Look what I found!" That such tiny white buds could effuse such a powerful smell and with it such poignant memories justified an afternoon of all of us offering advice on how this plant could survive a New York winter.

The Yard

The jasmine tree served many purposes.

Candy was the upstairs neighbours' teenage daughter. Her suitors would dim their car lights and the leaves of the tree would offer better protection for the lovers. In days before the "missed call" and "please call me", a tiny little hoot was the only way to communicate to your date that you had arrived. It would have to be an innocuous hoot. An intentional hoot would have every family peep through their curtains like meerkats and a half-hearted hoot would mean that you could be sitting there all night. Candy's boyfriends had it down to a fine art. Her family lived diagonally opposite Ma's flat upstairs. She was beautiful, giggly, often silly, and we all aspired to be like her. She could colour code her outfits like no-one else: deep purple and shocking pink, neon green and psychedelic yellow, a scarf clumsily tied into her long hair and rows of plastic bangles. The miniskirt was made of stretch fabric and she would adjust it just as she was about to descend the flight of stairs. We were in awe. The original Madonna. Ma's kitchen window offered a good view of her rushing down into the waiting car whose lights shone on her as she flew down the stairs before her father noticed her absence. It was like a spotlight on an actor. We trained our ears to listen out for the innocuous hoot and rushed to the dark kitchen and pushed and shoved each other out of the way to get a glimpse of her latest ensemble.

We did not tire of this drill. It was a ritual that all the girl cousins shared. Candy was an enigma. We never saw her during the day, which made her all the more alluring. She did not do chores, which made her an *Übermensch*. One

Friday night we heard the tiny little hoot and we all scrambled to get to the kitchen window. As we were shushing each other, the staircase lit up even brighter and there was another tiny little hoot! We were stunned. Why would he hoot twice? We saw Candy shut the kitchen door and start her descent down the runway, but she was more brightly lit than she had ever been. Then it dawned on us. She had double-booked. We all held our breath. Two suitors, two cars and one Candy. She stopped at the base of the stairs, smiled her most charming smile, turned around and sashayed her way back up. Slowly and deliberately. That was Candy. It could have been my age – I was 12 at the time – but that walk up the stairs rivals every other iconic moment of owning one's self without apology. Nobody knows what happened to the family after they relocated to Lenasia and I am thankful for that. In my mind, Candy will always be 19 years old.

Then there was Nitesh. Nitesh belonged to a wealthy Hindu family who lived in a flat directly above Ma's. He was a caricature of the villain in every Bollywood movie I have ever seen. Hairy, unkempt, his uniform was stone-washed jeans and a thin black belt which served no purpose. He would team this with a white vest that struggled to contain the hair on his body. It peeked out of every opening of the vest. He would drive into the Yard with a loud bash of the front left headlight and then screech to a halt outside his flat, sending the gravel and pebbles flying. Always in a foul mood, he would slam his car door shut and start fulminating at his mother or sisters. I learnt how to swear in Gujarati from Nitesh. The monologue would start, "Why is the roti cold, why is the roti hot, why is the house cold, why is the house hot, why is the shirt creased ..." It was mainly about the quality of the roti, though. Someone who pronounces the name for the unleavened bread as "rooti" not "rawti" could never understand Nitesh's frustration.

A well-made roti has layers of *pur* which can only be achieved by adding splashes of ghee and oil to the flour and folding the dough in half, then into quarters, then rolling it round again before slapping it onto a hot *tawah*, a large flat pan, often blackened from years of use. If you have completed every step perfectly, you are gifted a roti that swells and puffs as the layers of ghee seep through with the heat. An experienced hand slides it off the *tawah* and slaps it back down with a final flourish of ghee. The speckles of brown should be evenly distributed, achieved by spinning it on the *tawah*. Theoretically, I know how roti is made.

Our family would sometimes eat supper in silence listening to the latest tirade coming from upstairs. Ma commented once that he terrorised his family. We all nodded in agreement. An only son, he was worshipped by his family. As a young adult, his temper tantrums and rage were fuelled by the fact that all the women to whom he proposed marriage ended up turning him down. The loud intrusions eventually lost entertainment value and Ma allowed us to take a broom and knock on the ceiling to signal to the family above that we had had enough of Nitesh. This worked for a week and then he just ignored us. In fact, on one occasion he lifted what sounded like a chair and banged it on the floor of his flat. *Screw you*, the chair communicated.

Apart from the tirades, very little verified information

came our way. The most reliable source of information was their domestic helper, Gloria. She had relocated from Mpumalanga and had a piece-job at the Daya family home. She would do laundry, iron and scrub the *tawah* every second day. On days when Nitesh was at his worst, she would stop at the bottom of the stairs and spit with disgust. She and Ma would meet at the concrete laundry basins and conduct long conversations in Afrikaans. Sometimes, while Ma did laundry, Gloria would sit in the sun and eat watered-down dhal and brown bread from an enamel plate. Ma was born in Groot Marico, so Gujarati was her first language, Afrikaans her second and English her third. Gloria had a favourite idiom and almost every conversation with Ma about Nitesh ended with her saying, "One day is one day". I remember going to my well-used orange *Students' Companion* to look up this expression. I could not find it. The House of Delegates English curriculum – designed especially for Indian schoolchildren, as opposed to White or Black – shoved Christian morality down our throats and we would say things like "Cleanliness is next to godliness" and "Silence is golden" and "Empty vessels make the most noise". The curriculum really sucked the joy out of the language.

    I digress. Nitesh Daya was the heir to an empire of potato farms and a fleet of trucks. My description of the way in which he ran the family business simplified the term "exploitation" for my 12-year-old son. Every morning, he would rise 15 minutes after the muezzin had called worshippers, counselling them that prayer is better than sleep. He would go over to the garage that housed all the family's

The Yard

trucks and start them all to warm them up. He would then go back to bed until 8.30am, leaving all the residents in the Yard to wake up to fumes from the diesel engines. By this time there was a queue of about 40 African men hoping for a piece-job on the day. Nitesh had no rate that he paid for the day. The length of the queue was inversely proportionate to his daily rate. He would taunt and humiliate them as he walked down the queue picking his labourers for the day.

"So old you are, you older than my grandfather!"

"You look very clever; I don't want clever boys working here!"

"You look like a tsotsi, going to steal all my potatoes!"

The work was difficult. When trucks arrived from the farms, labourers had to load smaller trucks using wheelbarrows and spades. Nitesh wanted the work done in record time so that he could dedicate the day to harassing his family.

He would sometimes promise those he did not choose for the day that they could have the potatoes that were not fit for sale. By midday, a handful would wait around and he would relish telling them that God was good, not a single potato was unfit. Of course, word spread that he hardly kept his promise so he would, on occasion, part with a little packet of soft, rotting potatoes to keep his game alive.

Needless to say, Nitesh could not find a woman willing to marry him. Despite the effort Aunty Nirmala put into getting him to oil down his hair and wear a shirt, his Sunday afternoon proposals were in vain. His miserable demeanour made sure of that. There was plenty of opportunity for proposing – it was considered bad manners not to allow a family to visit and propose, probably because it might send the unintended message to the community that the young woman did not want to settle down. (Yes, I understand the implications of thinking that she was unsettled until she was married. It evokes images of an agitated, imbalanced female does it not? The only word that I think does one better is to call the groom's party the *jaan*, which means "the life". After being unsettled, the life comes back into you. You have to love that.)

When I was about ten, his mum decided to fly to India with him and make a financially viable offer to a fair-skinned woman from a poor family who had birthed a daughter trained in the art of roti-making. He sat with a sullen expression on his face in the olive-green Mercedes-Benz listening to his Walkman while his mum packed his suitcase and his father, Uncle Bavesh, carried it down the stairs to take them to the airport. Aunty Nirmala climbed into the back seat and passed him a *bhiroo*, a rolled up roti with a meat or potato filling, as padkos for the journey to the airport. One would think that with Nitesh in such a volatile mood, she would play it safe and make a sandwich instead. A roti-roll it was and they set off.

In the two weeks that followed, talk of Nitesh's new wife reached fever pitch in the Yard. Everyone had an opinion about the miserable life the young woman would lead in exchange for her family being paid a generous dowry. How would Nirmala feel if one of her daughters married a man like Nitesh? The general feeling was that Nirmala did not want to be in the direct line of fire so she was taking another man's

The Yard

daughter and bringing her to a home of hell. It is a typically Indian expression. When a woman is seen in relation to a man in her family, then and only then do we empathise with her circumstances. Only when she is some man's daughter, some man's sister, some man's granddaughter.

Actually, she was herself. She was Sapna and the Yard was about to meet her.

One day, Nitesh and Nirmala returned to the Yard in a taxi. The driver banged the front left bumper and parked outside the flat. Dozens of curious eyes peeked through voile, lace and chiffon curtains to form a first impression of the new bride. Sapna's skin tone and the inexpensive cotton *punjabi* with very little embroidery that she was wearing confirmed what the residents had already bet on. She jumped out of the car first and looked around, taking in her new surroundings. She stretched her arms out to shake off the exhaustion and then noticed her father-in-law at the foot of the stairs. Respectfully, she bounced over to him and touched his feet and he bent down and held her shoulders limply as if to say, "Don't worry about the formalities," but we all knew that nothing less was expected. Next, she grabbed him and threw her arms around him in a bear hug. Holes were bored into voile curtains at this point. She hooked her arm into his and started up the stairs.

"Where's *bhen* (sister)?" we heard her say before she disappeared into the flat. Nitesh and Aunty Nirmala were left to carry the bags upstairs. Sapna did not bother looking back. We could hardly wait for Gloria to come back the following day and deliver an intelligence report.

A HOME ON VORSTER STREET

It was a full 48 hours later that we heard Nitesh start up again. Gloria had not been back downstairs to do laundry and all we could do was speculate on how Sapna was settling down.

Hearing Nitesh complaining, Ma wryly remarked, "Even girls from India can't please him."

Suddenly, we heard a commotion from upstairs. No voices, it sounded like a pile of dishes had fallen. And then silence. Nobody came down.

Ma wrung her hands in anticipation of Gloria leaving at 5pm. Luckily, *Maghrib* prayers would not clash with her plan. It was summer, which meant that the sun would set much later.

Accosted, Gloria shook her head. "Sapna? He eh eh, that one ..." but her self-satisfied smile had us bursting with curiosity. Gloria had finished work late and would miss the Putco bus if she stayed, but she promised a full debrief the following day.

Ma had never been so eager to tackle laundry. Gloria relayed the story slowly.

Sapna had started making roti for lunch the previous day with Nitesh micro-managing the process from the dining-room table. Of course, we all knew that it was a stream of criticism rather than constructive input, his hands had never touched flour. Gloria got more animated, she was working the Omo into a flourish of lather, aware of having Ma's attention but not making eye-contact.

"*Dan sê hy, 'Gooi meer botter,' dan gooi sy meer, dan skree hy weer, dan begin sy weer ... Yoh Ouma ... dan SLAAN sy hom met daardie swart pan! Op sy KOP, Ouma! Dan het*

The Yard

Madam begin lag, dan het Baas begin lag ... en ek het vir jou gesê ... one day is one day!"[1]

Gloria's story was so outrageous that it was hardly believable. Within the hour, Ma had told Khala-next-door who told Aunty Yasmin who worked at Dharee Wara's grocery store and by nightfall this story was being discussed in the homes of all the women that Nitesh had proposed to. The community was abuzz.

The turban around Nitesh's forehead the next morning confirmed the story. His brash quick walk had become round-shouldered and he took the steps up to the flat slowly. Occasionally we would see Sapna having her lunch in the sun with Gloria and trying out smatterings of Afrikaans. She would always be laughing and joyful and animated. She had insulated herself from years of verbal abuse with one swing of a frying pan. There is a Gujarati word that sums up Nitesh's new demeanour: *hiddoh* – straighten out.

Unlike with Candy, I know what happened to Nitesh. When he was three months away from becoming a father, the family bought a string of motels and relocated to Texas. Sapna bade a tearful goodbye to Gloria in fluent Afrikaans and hugged her tightly. In my mind, she now runs a chain of motels and Nitesh's voice has been permanently lowered to a barely audible whisper. Wherever they are, I know that she is happy.

---

[1] "Then he says, 'Add more butter,' which she does, then he screams again, so she begins again ... Wow, Grandma, at that she hits him with that black griddle! On the head, Grandma! Then madam began laughing, then the boss began laughing ... I've always told you ... one day is one day!"

Chapter 5

Favourite Favourite

Salim was the chocolate wrapped in purple cellophane in a box of Quality Street, he was everybody's "favourite-favourite". Bajee, Ma and Khala-next-door all fell hopelessly in love with this scrawny baby. So did my mum, as yet unmarried and still living in Vorster Street.

The thing about favourites is that one has little control over how they are selected. It is like asking a person to explain why they prefer pears to apples; it is very difficult to articulate with any certainty.

It was not the birthing order; he was one of Papa and Gorimummy's middle children, the second of five siblings. It wasn't that he was a boy; he had an older and a younger brother. It certainly was not his personality as he was born scowling. My mum's favourite nephew, she still describes his sullenness with pride, as though he had a right to behave that way, well, because he was the favourite-favourite.

"He was a little SHIT!" My mum would beam, in a way that made one think it was something to be aspired to.

Every grandchild was treated equally, except Salim. At the end of every week, ten metres before he reached the polished red stoep on Vorster Street, Bajee would call his name, arm outstretched, holding a brown paper package full of Nut Puffs, Wilson's boiled sweets and, of course, Chappies.

Salim would bounce up to his adoring grandfather and graciously accept the bag. "Sweets! Sweets! Look at what I have!"

I have heard from my older cousins that this scene played itself out week after week, year after year. I often think that it would have felt deeply unfair if there had been just two or three grandchildren. As it was, there were so many that the injustice was shared equally. Nobody had the audacity to ask Bajee what his intention was in handing the package to Salim.

"Just one, Salim, please."

He would shake his head and explain that he truly wished he could share, but had Bajee wanted them to partake, he would have bought them their own stash. They could, however, watch him eat. A game of Ludo or pick-up-sticks would pause while he unwrapped a Chappies and popped it into his mouth. The smell of pink Chappies rubbed his position as the favourite-favourite into their noses.

Salim's *paan* was easily distinguishable from the pile of betel nut leaf prepared by Khala-next-door. It was the fattest of the lot, thick with love. The leaf would drip pink rivulets onto his white school shirt and the sweet taste of *saumph*, fennel seed, would burst out as an expression of her adoration.

When the deadbolts, which we called *starprees*, were shut for the evening and everyone went to bed, he would saunter over to my mum and climb onto her lap. Wordlessly, she would lift him in her arms and rock him to sleep, swaying quietly in the dark while humming a tune from a Hindi movie. Occasionally, she would look at his face to check if he had fallen asleep to relieve her numb arm, but his frown was a signal for her to continue the nocturnal dance. It could take up to two hours, but it didn't matter. It was Salim.

His older sibling Hanif had inherited Bajee's physique, and Salim, being younger and half of Hanif's height and width, was no match in a punch-up. Hanif, true to his magnanimous temperament and partially out of respect for Bajee, would rarely strike back, choosing instead to hold out his arms to deflect Salim's onslaught.

"*Eneh noh chere!*" Bajee's booming voice would warn the recipient of Salim's temper not to needle him, leaving no doubt whose side he was on.

Salim would cry nonetheless, his inflated ego frustrated by his inability to inflict any meaningful damage. My mum, having witnessed these exchanges countless times, took Salim aside and, motivated by fear of Salim harming himself by running into his brother at full speed, explained that, in time, he would grow and be able to have a "fair go" at his brother. For now it would be best to leave Hanif alone. But as a boxing trainer would motivate their star, she suggested jumping exercises to help the much-anticipated growth spurt along.

Salim took to running down the short passage at full speed and then trying to touch the top of the low doorframe with his hands. He would practise for hours, the passage expropriated for his exclusive use. The rest of the family would duck in and out of rooms to avoid colliding with him. He got so good that on one occasion, he jumped so high that he knocked his forehead against the frame and passed out in the passage. The family's primary concern was explaining to Bajee how Salim managed to injure himself when there were so many seemingly responsible adults around. His own stupidity and stubbornness were beyond question.

Salim's transition into adulthood attracted a new, more sinister interest. In the early 1970s he would become the favourite-favourite of the Security Branch.

The bright red T-shirt with a raised fist initially caused the most problems: "Workers of the World Unite!" The colour bled into all the laundry. Occasionally, it would be a yellow T-shirt hanging between the school uniforms and drying in the winds of change.

While all of us were aware of the systematic exploitation of apartheid, this family that lived on Vorster Street raised more than one child who believed, with everything he had, that the system could and would be destroyed by organised activism. Salim was following in the footsteps of his older brother – the sense of justice that had stopped the young Hanif from punching his younger brother had also turned him into an activist.

Salim spent less and less time at home. Annoying his

cousins became a distant memory, replaced by a commitment which he has spent the rest of his life honouring.

Salim noticed his father's vile mood when he had to walk seven kilometres home from work when there was public transport available – but not for him. The buses, all in mint condition, could hold 70 people, but would drive past Papa with a handful of privileged individuals, laughing and oblivious to his exhaustion. He counted 12 passing him on one walk home. An extraordinarily gifted cricketer, Papa was forced to leave school at 16 to help support the family and ensure that his five siblings were educated. When the family sat around the supper table, Salim would silently take note of the times his father described being called a "coolie".

He would sit on his haunches, deep in thought, hand his grandmother the green Sunlight bar and observe her wash, hang and iron clothes for the railway workers' wives in Fietas. He was a pageboy for most of his aunts, all of whom married young in a conspiracy of patriarchy and apartheid. Talented, intelligent women with no opportunities to make a meaningful mark on society. He watched his older cousins boarding a rickety bus filled to capacity from Newtown to Roodepoort because there was no high school in the area. His four cousins from Lichtenburg moved into Vorster Street because there was no high school for them within a 200-kilometre radius. There were four high schools in Lichtenburg, but none an Indian child could attend.

His activism was ignited by everything and everyone.

From about 1974 Captain Sons and Detective Harrypersadh of the Security Branch were charged with keeping a close eye on Salim. They would bang on the door urgently,

Favourite Favourite

at all hours of the day and night, looking for him. (They would come looking for Hanif too, until he was detained for a year in Modderbee prison.) Salim was often not at home and their combined frustration would leave the small flat messy and dishevelled. If he was home, they would simply arrest him – he was arrested about 14 times in the decade. He never went quietly, but the brutality with which he was thrown into the yellow police van would leave the family and the community stunned for several seconds after they had left for John Vorster Square Police Station. Neighbours would draw their teenage sons closer, fearful that Salim's spirit would inspire their own sons down the path of damnation. Some families in the community built empires on the shoulders of apartheid and other families still deal with the tragic psychological consequences of an encounter with the Security Branch.

On one particular occasion, they banged on the door so frantically that the rusty *starpree* unhinged and the door hung from the frame, defeated in the face of barbarity. Ma rose slowly. This was unusual; it was usually Papa or any adult male who happened to be home who dealt with them. Bajee had passed on and Ma was now permanently on crutches after having broken her hip. She rose from her bed and opened the door. Harrypersadh, not expecting to see the grandmother of the house looking up at him, addressed her in Gujarati. "Ma, Salim *ka che* – Ma, where is Salim?"

She stepped back to raise one crutch to his face and said to him, "I am NOT your mother. YOUR mother must be ASHAMED of you."

It was a quiet courage that Ma had, a steely one nonetheless. The more exposure the family had to the Security Branch, the greater the support for Salim grew. He was never asked to justify the Cause.

When word reached the family two kilometres away from John Vorster Square Police Station that Salim was being held, everyone would walk there. Nobody there could confirm whether or not Salim Vally was being held. Nobody could confirm if he had been charged. The family was aware that he could be held for months without being charged. Nobody could confirm if he had indeed been arrested. We could bring food which might or might not be given to him. Had he been interrogated? He was just 15 years old that year, 1975. The investigating officer could never remember these minor details.

"*Salim Vally is 'n groot cleva.*" This much he remembered to say to the family.

The family organised. My family learnt quickly that if they screamed his name in unison, on a count of three, he would wave out of the window of the ninth floor to prove that he was alive. His mother would cry with relief.

Food is love and triple the usual amount had to be prepared in the hope that if the family fed the investigating officer who was suffering from amnesia, it would jog his memory and he would pass some on to Salim. The family gave the officer too much credit. Samoosas prepared by the family were indeed enjoyed by the Security Police, but the leftovers were squashed in front of detainees. Sometimes, the detainees would be forced to clean the mess after torture by electric shock. Salim always spared the family the details of his time at John Vorster.

Favourite Favourite

At other times, the Security Police would allow a window of half an hour in which to bring food and then, having enjoyed the samoosas of another family earlier, would insist that the delivery had arrived after the deadline and refuse to take the parcel. It would sit on the kitchen counter, everyone having lost their appetite, and Ma would sob silently in her prayers as she swung her head from side to side in greeting the angels sitting on each shoulder. Prayer and food were interludes in an ominous atmosphere whenever he was detained.

Being caught with material relating to gatherings meant five years' imprisonment. In December of 1976 Salim opened the front door of the house wearing a winter jacket bulging with pamphlets. The material was about a commemoration of the Soweto Uprisings earlier that year. Sitting across the road were Harrypersadh and Sons. Quickly calculating his options, Salim closed the door gently behind him and started walking down Vorster Street towards Fietas, aware that they had now risen from the pavement and begun sauntering behind him.

He walked to Fietas, snaking the roads, greeting familiar faces but feeling the eyes bearing down on him. The urgency of dumping the material must have been unbearable but Salim continued to walk and they continued to hunt him. Eventually, he walked to the Oriental Plaza and into my parents' shop. The Security Branch waited outside, knowing that as soon as he left they would arrest him and find something in that small shop that would send him away for five years. They could hardly wait. They had cornered their prey and were rubbing their sweaty hands in anticipation of the triumph.

A HOME ON VORSTER STREET

I had been born in January of 1976. I was unsteady on my feet, crawling around the little shop. On seeing Salim, I sat on my knees and lifted my arms to be thrown into the air. It was something boy cousins did. The girl cousins would pinch my cheeks. He lifted me up and threw me into the air, depositing a hundred A5 pamphlets between my cloth nappy and my waterproof. (The latter was a hard, plastic nappy with bad-tempered elastics which created welts around the upper thighs of chubby toddlers. It could easily have been a torture device but every baby wore one at the time.)

They demolished that shop. They emptied baby formula, turned the cot out, removed goods from the shelves, partially stripped the carpet and terrorised my mother. Grudgingly they let Salim go after a few painful smacks to quell their bitterness and disbelief that their tip-off had not resulted in a conviction. Had the pamphlets been found, I don't doubt that they would have arrested me, along with my mother.

In 2002 Salim was arrested for allegedly contravening the Regulation of Gatherings Act. At the time, he was the Acting Director of the Wits Education Policy Unit and was attempting to get to his office at the Johannesburg College of Education, now the Wits School of Education. He was denied access, as the Jewish Board of Deputies had been given control of the campus while they hosted Shimon Peres, the Zionist politician, later president of Israel. As an employee of the university, Salim demanded access, was assaulted by security and was unceremoniously thrown into the back of a police van and arrested.

Favourite Favourite

Eighteen supporters who marched to the Hillbrow Police Station to demand his release were also arrested. The hourly news updates on Talk Radio 702 carried the story and within the hour, the family knew of Salim's arrest.

As they approached an embankment, before the police station came into sight, they heard the unmistakable sound of people who knew that they were on the right side of history.

Hundreds of comrades, students, activists, trade unionists, politicians, lawyers, NGOs and colleagues were singing struggle songs and waving Palestinian flags in solidarity and demanding Salim's release. There was no need for samoosas anymore; he had some of the best legal minds in Johannesburg jostling with each other to arrange his release.

We watched from a distance. There was no need to go any closer. Professor Salim Vally was everyone's favourite-favourite.

Chapter 6

What's in a Name?

Can a person live an entire lifetime without anybody knowing what their given name is? Surely, a person needs to hear their name. Degrees of familiarity and affection are determined by the tone in which your name is called. What's in a name? Everything.

All of my life, Khala was my granny's neighbour. All the grandchildren eventually called her Khala-next-door as if that was her birth name. Her identity was a suffix, determined in physical terms, to the root word. We said it in one word. Who came by to visit? Khala-next-door.

I had not given much thought to Khala-next-door in the last 20 years until one day recently. I was walking down Mint Road in Fordsburg and came across the cart of the *paan walla* – the betel nut leaf seller. The cart was basic, with no

What's in a Name?

wheels, which made me wonder how it got there. The rectangular chipboard held together with drawing pins and the name of the cart, "Ansaar Paan", proudly spray-painted on the front panel. I had walked past this very cart many times before but the Consol jar holding the candy-coated *saumph* caught my eye and I hesitated. The vendor looked at me, lazily chewing his wares, and like a seasoned pro I said, "Everything".

He barely nodded but began constructing the *paan*: betel leaf, *supari*, the all-important candy sweets, rose syrup and three more ingredients, all eventually tightly packed into a triangle and double-wrapped in cling film and then newspaper. He seemed satisfied that I could appreciate an authentic *mithi paan* without wasting his time asking what each item was. Reminding myself that I was born in this area and had therefore probably built some resistance to any bacteria lurking in his greasy containers, my thoughts were interrupted by memories of Khala-next-door.

In her tiny three-roomed apartment, the fridge was a podium on which the *paan dabbo*, the container for the betel nut leaf, rested. Hand-engraved Indian blossoms were etched into the ornate lid, which housed seven little silver bowls, each with a different flavour. Next to the *paan dabbo*, slightly to the left, was a brass tin of Mazawattee tea. The vintage tin had an image of an old lady with black-rimmed glasses and a younger child enjoying a cup of tea. To the right of the *paan dabbo* was a purple velvet box, which housed something of incredible value to Khala. It was never opened and even as children we had the presence of mind never to ask. Like the winners' podium at a Formula One

Race, the top of Khala's fridge was a shrine to everything that was of value to her.

If we visited Khala, we were guaranteed three things: a tightly packed syrupy *paan*, a portion of a packet of pink Romantics sweets and your name being hopelessly massacred. One could hardly blame her; it seemed that there was no end to grandchildren spewing out of Ma's house. My name, fairly common these days, became "Raageena". My cousin Shameela's name was given an altogether more exotic twist, "Sharrrrmila", and my cousin Tashmia was simply "Rasid-Ahmed's *motti pooirie*" – his eldest daughter. One could hardly blame her.

Names, like everything else in life, follow trends and South African Muslim names are no exception. The moody teenage grandchildren would correct Khala, while the toddlers and young adults had the maturity to let this slide. Khala would just laugh at our "fancy-fancy" names and we were never in any doubt about who she was referring to when we got summoned. As Ma's "sister" she would have an all-too-often ignored vote in naming new grandchildren. To be fair, Ma was wholly ignored too. These were the 1970s, so while my aunts were not burning their bras or smoking weed, the anti-establishment atmosphere made itself felt when their children were named. Simply put, they chose names with a Persian root word rather than an Arabic root word. For those who are unfamiliar with either language, my aunts replaced names such as "Abigail", "Elizabeth" and "Rachel" with the equivalent of "Skylar", "Taylor" and "Luna".

Khala visited Ma every afternoon. She would enter from

What's in a Name?

the Yard, coming through the kitchen door. The door was never locked during the day – doors were only closed and "*starpreed*" when the last occupant of the house retired for the night. Often, these brass slots were attached to the doors by two rusty nails, jarred loose from the frame by sibling arguments over time. A new *starpree* was stiff, requiring violent manoeuvring up and down to loosen while pushing one's entire body weight on the door to line it up with the frame. Well-worn ones would slide effortlessly and in tune to the muezzin clearing his throat at dawn for *Fajr salah*.

Even before that day in Mint Road I had resolved to ask my mum what had happened to her. I knew that Khala must have passed on: she was about 75 years old when our family left Fordsburg. Each chew of the *paan* brought back more memories of Khala.

I unlocked my car and jumped in. The silence was welcome, compared to the vibrant Indian music and melodious *nazms* of the street. I sat absolutely still with a pounding headache watching the car guard in the rear-view mirror. It was a Saturday: many kitchens in homes were closed for the day and this parking bay situated in prime property opposite Akhalwaya's take-aways would be greatly sought after.

Ha! I had told the *paan walla* to add "everything" and that included a generous heap of tobacco which in combination with the betel leaf is known for its psychoactive and stimulant properties. That would probably explain the hours of conspiring with cousins about who would visit Khala and pluck up enough courage to ask for *paan*. We loved HER *paan* and now I knew why.

She had a little peephole in her door so that she could

see who was knocking without opening the door. We were all under ten, so when we visited one cousin had to hold another cousin up so that Khala could see that it was someone familiar. Her stoep on Vorster Street was always polished bright red and slippery so one had to be incredibly careful about hoisting one's baby cousin. One wrong move and we'd all come crashing down. The knock required three participants. One to knock and scream her name, usually the brainchild behind the operation. The second to stand steady, legs buckling under the weight. The third just had to hold on to the shoulders of the second and grin. The instruction was to HOLD ON TO THE SHOULDERS but we generally grabbed each other's braided hair like a horse's reins. I had at different times in my childhood assumed each of these roles – and there is nothing quite as painful as waiting for an elderly woman to heed your calls while every strand of your hair is being pulled by chunky, sticky hands. It was a rite of passage to be the one hoisted to grin at Khala. You would be "on" until the next unsuspecting baby was old enough for the succession plan.

Khala's visits to our flat intensified with the advent of VHS tapes. Family members would hire the latest Hindi movie and Ma and Khala would wait patiently for a grandchild to come home from school or university and rewind the cassette, fast-forward the Hindu prayers at the beginning and then press play just as the title began. A momentary check with each other around midday to make sure that the *Zuhr* prayers had been performed and then they were good to go until the *Asr Salaat* prayers in the late afternoon. Until we showed Ma the fast-forward button, she and Khala

What's in a Name?

viewed many movies only partially, because under no circumstances could the movie compete with the muezzin. Once Ma learnt how to use fast-forward, it was usually the song and dance garden scenes that got ditched. It was quite something to see her. She got so good she could hit the button just as the actors started staring intently at each other, even before the first note of the inevitable song.

Khala, not being *au fait* with the Bollywood movie industry and their ability to produce 800 movies a year, would sometimes confuse the storylines and the actors. It was admittedly difficult to keep up with the number of times Amitabh Bachchan died. She would view these as a continuum and this led to some hilarious conversations between her and Ma.

Khala: "He is living again? Yesterday he died."

Ma: "That was yesterday. Today he is alive."

Indian movies of the 1980s were already a precursor for the salacious storylines of the later movies, and the two elderly women watched a few of them in utter disgust before concluding that they were wasting their time.

There was one condition for any of the grandchildren watching an Indian movie with them. One had to dish a plate of food from the ever-present pot on the stove, an admission ticket of sorts. The movie would be interrupted countless times by her pleas to go and dish up. Both Ma and Khala would be distracted by the fact that you had joined them without bringing a plate of food and they would take turns to gently remind you. Ma was the Queen of Resourceful. Wednesdays saw a dish we called "surprise rice", largely made up of leftovers from the preceding week. We quickly learnt to stop dissecting the dish and wondering when last all the elements had been presented separately. Since Ma's passing I have yet to taste anything so delicious.

—

Ignoring the car guard's pleas for me to move, I dialled my mum.

"Howzit mummy, what are you doing?" I have called my mum every morning at 9am for the twenty years since I left her home to get married. Those words are always the opening. For 11 months of the year her answer is "drinking tea". Tea is more than a warm beverage for my mum. The kettle gets boiled before important decisions are made, in the face of tragedy or even to coax a way forward out of her. It's very common for my mum to say, "Wait, I cannot think, I need tea."

Grateful that her drug was on hand, I asked her about Khala.

Khala-next-door was the third wife to a wealthy businessman in India. He was 65 when they married, she was 15. To her parents, living in dire poverty, the marriage offer required very little thought. The age gap between the suitor and their only daughter was not considered. Nor was the fact that their daughter would be his third wife. Khala's husband Cha-Cha and his two wives were sickly and she fulfilled the role of hard-working domestic helper, dedicated nurse and loyal caretaker to all three pensioners. The first and second wives passed on in India and Khala's husband thought it an opportune time to move to South Africa. He was, by then, nearly 70 and she was barely 20.

What's in a Name?

For the next few winters, Cha-Cha's extended family chose to visit South Africa during the Indian summer to escape the oppressive heat. I don't think that they bargained for a Highveld winter. Khala made these visits bearable for them by preparing fresh *adoo-pak*, the ginger and nut mix famous for warming the body from the inside. After breakfast, she would rub the feet of the eldest members of the family with Zam-Buk to improve circulation and prevent chilblains. The guests' bodies were simply not equipped to withstand the bitterly cold weather but Khala did everything a daughter-in-law of a traditional home could do to make them comfortable.

Parties of 15 relatives would visit for three months at a time and they had to be fed three meals a day. Washing was laundered by hand and Khala would brave the wind at 5am, dumping the dirty clothes into a large steel bin with frozen fingers, retrieving the green bar of Sunlight soap from the pocket of her morning dress. Once this was done, she would disappear into her home, only to be seen the next morning on laundry duty again. They would eventually leave, just as the mornings became less frosty and spring blossoms began budding. Nobody would hear from them for a year. They would visit again, less one or two elderly members but with several babies and, as a result, considerably more laundry than the previous year.

Cha-Cha was a wealthy man, so the items to prepare the food and the Sunlight bars could be purchased without much difficulty out of the money that he gave her for their upkeep each week. Out of reverence for her in-laws, Khala never bought processed items of food. She chose to make every meal from scratch. She would patiently roast *dhania* over a wood-burning stove and pound ginger and garlic fresh every day. The labour involved did not even cross her mind. She was content and grateful to be the wife of a man whose mouth housed a complete set of gold teeth.

The three-metre stoep on Vorster Street had a front door. Visitors walked without knocking into a lounge which led directly into a bedroom which led directly into a kitchen with a backdoor. It was possible to move from one end of the house to the other in five giant leaps. Toilets and showers were communal, located outside. Their furniture was an assortment of unmatched items, each covered in different floral prints to preserve the original upholstered fabric. Coffee tables and counter tops were draped with numerous crocheted tea cloths and the walls were covered in bright blue bouquets of wallpaper. The curtains were heavy chocolate brown velvet. The effect was a schizophrenic room closing in on itself.

Khala did fall pregnant once but miscarried late in her pregnancy. She and Cha-Cha were silently devastated, neither sharing their grief with the other. Cha-Cha's health deteriorated rapidly after that. She nursed him as she had his wives, stoically, not making plans for herself or asking questions about their finances or how she would survive without the weekly brown envelope of money.

I had to ask my mother, "What happened to Cha-Cha's gold teeth when he died?"

My mum said, deadpan, "They were removed with pliers before the *ghusal* and kept on top of her fridge in a purple velvet box."

What's in a Name?

The *ghusal* is the Muslim rite of bathing a body before burial. Why did I ask?

Khala was left with no known family in South Africa and no real inclination to return to India. She was a 22-year-old widow whose husband left all his wealth in the hands of trustees to manage. She was illiterate, unable to speak English and a very wealthy woman. My mum spoke of the difficulties she had in having small amounts of money released to her. While it took care of rental, water and electrical accounts, her monthly stipend belied the bank account balance left for her by Cha-Cha. Funds to satisfy cravings for almonds for *badaam* milk would take up to a month to satisfy. Hardly a dent was made in his account from his death to hers.

I remember Khala as being talkative, jovial even, of slight build and always wearing broad cream pants, socks with sandals and a mismatched long shapeless dress hanging longer in front with each passing year as osteoporosis set in. Her mouth perpetually red and leaving the liquorice scent of betel leaves hanging in a room long after she had left.

—

The early 1990s saw a mass exodus as some families from Vorster Street, including Papa and Gorimummy, moved to Lenasia and Mayfair. Others moved to Homestead Park. These new homes, former railway workers' homes, had gardens and were palaces compared to the flats in Fordsburg. The nuclear family was born.

Starprees had been shut forever.

Ma stayed on in Vorster Street for a while, now living

with her daughter Zubeda, although they would also move out soon. I would like to think Khala made a brave decision to continue to stay in Vorster Street, but she did not have many options. By now Ma was too old to take practical care of her lifelong friend, so Mum phoned her regularly, checking on her every second day to deliver milk and bread. DairyBelle had suspended their door-to-door milk delivery service.

It was difficult to pick up the emptiness during the day because former residents of Fordsburg still worked in the area, but the evenings gave way to an eerie silence.

And without the hustle and bustle of a busy community, Fordsburg in the early hours of the morning was creepy. It could have been the way the moon shone against Newtown Mosque's minaret, silhouetting bats hunting for the discarded contents of the previous day's tiffins. It could also be the far more sinister reputation Vorster Street has for housing other-worldly creatures. Stories abound from devout worshippers being approached by men who disappear into thin air to Qurans being opened and closed by invisible hands, sudden gusts of wind sweeping through the mosque when the doors are closed, and strange knocks and taps in the night. These incidents ensured that men never visited the mosque alone.

Towards the end of Khala's life, the loneliness and, to some extent, sheer heartache of her life led to episodes of dementia. Only a week before they moved to Mayfair West my parents, who still lived three blocks away, received a chilling call at about 1am. It was from one of the few remaining residents of the Yard saying that she was throwing her

What's in a Name?

furniture and coins into the street and screaming at nobody in particular. My parents rushed over on foot down Pine Avenue, up Malherbe Street and into Vorster Street, which is a long street, with flats on either side, ending in the T-junction with Newtown Mosque. In the middle of the street was Khala, in her night clothes, talking animatedly and oblivious to the temperature, which was below freezing.

"Julie! *Ya* Allah! I have asked them again and again and they don't want to listen."

"Who? Khala? What are you talking about?"

"All these visitors came to my house after the *Isha* prayers and they say that they are going to live with me. I told them that they can't but they just won't listen. I'm throwing everything out of the house so they will have to leave."

My parents, in complete shock and expecting to confront a group of squatters, threw a blanket over Khala and ushered her into the flat. Not a soul in sight. There was a dim light on in the lounge, her bedroom in darkness and the kitchen light flickering on and off.

"Where, Khala, what are you talking about? There's nobody here."

"Julie! That man is almost sitting in your lap. He is the most stubborn, sitting there and laughing at me."

What would I have given to have seen my mum's face!

"These children also, they are EVERYWHERE, running and jumping on my furniture. Their mother is sitting in THAT corner on the floor with the burka and *tasbeeh* but she won't even look up!" Khala was pointing at the kitchen.

To increase the drama, the bulb finally expired.

"See? She switched the light off; she thinks I can't see her!"

My parents were stunned. Khala continued ranting, occasionally swearing at the man to my mum's right. Then she started laughing.

"Julie, he says he wants to live with *you* but I told him that you are married. How *forward-forward* he is!"

I think it was the only time in 20 years that my mum held so tightly on to my dad's hand. My parents spoke to each other in Afrikaans because while Khala could not speak English, she could understand it well enough. After calming her down and holding mock conversations with unseen beings to appease her, my parents decided that she would spend the night at our home while my dad continued the negotiation with the visitors. Khala only agreed to accompany my mum home IF my dad spent the night at her place.

Now let me tell you about my dad. Nothing scares him. Horror movies are his favourite genre. He sat through *The Exorcist* in 1976 expressionless.

But he flat out refused to stay at Khala's on his own.

He followed them home at a distance. Realising that Khala needed round-the-clock care, my mum contacted the trustees, and Cha-Cha's brother's son from Laudium took Khala into their home that very week. She left Vorster Street with a small suitcase, the *paan dabbo* in one hand and the purple velvet box in the other. After she had been reassured that a non-existent delivery truck would follow with her furniture, Khala's *starpree* on Vorster Street was also bolted permanently.

Three weeks after our family's move to Mayfair West, my mum phoned the family Khala was living with to ask if she could visit and drop off an invitation to my wedding. This

What's in a Name?

was 2000, before cellphones had built-in navigation directions; you wrote on scraps of paper while balancing the receiver of the phone between your ear and shoulder. The plan was to hand-deliver invitations to family members, give a brief synopsis of my husband and gulp a cup of tea to ensure that nobody felt slighted by an unprocedural invitation. Depending on the size of one's wedding, this could take months.

It was nearing 8pm and my parents were hopelessly lost. They drove the length and breadth of Taj Street in Laudium, Pretoria West, where Khala now lived. The house was nowhere to be found.

My dad was typically short-tempered. "What kind of directions do you take, Julie?" he asked after half an hour of looking for the house.

"It's not my fault. The house is supposed to be here." She pointed at a random house. "It's not my fault that it's not HERE!" She pointed at another house.

They did eventually stop at a garage and ask. On finding the house they saw that it was in darkness. The family had decided to call it a night, activate the beams and slam-lock the Trellidor. Tired after a long day of niceties, my parents thought that they would return over the weekend to hand out the balance of invitations. They would make Khala their first stop.

Two days later, my mum received a call to say that Khala had passed away. On the day that my parents did not arrive, Khala had been up and showered by early morning and then sat on her bed like a bride, in a new dress and long gold chain, waiting until 9pm to receive my parents.

"I always told Khala to wear her new dresses; life is too short to save them."

—

By now the car guard had upped the tempo of his gestures to motivate me to leave his bay.

"What was her real name, Mummy?"

Suddenly, that was very important to me.

"Fatima. Her name was Fatima."

Chapter 7

Maverick

Maverick. That is the only word that comes to mind when I think of Khatija, my maternal aunt. As Ma used to say, no two fingers on one hand are the same and yet a mother loves all her children equally. If Khatija was a finger, she would be the index finger on the right hand. It is the finger used to hold knives steady and give direction. It is also the finger which is dipped into pots of food for tasting. The index finger has a maverick quality to it. That was Khatija.

Ma and Bajee had one son and then five daughters in quick succession. The age gap between the daughters bore testimony to their desperation for another son. In line with being a devout Muslim, Bajee's parenting skills extended to keeping his daughters off the front porch, out of view of the daily visitors to the mosque next door. He needn't have worried about prospective suitors as his physical appearance would have been enough to inspire the well-meaning to cross the road and arrive at the mosque making fervent *dua* that Ismail Vally did not spot him looking at his home. To round off his intimidating height and girth he had a Hitleresque moustache and black rimmed spectacles. The waistcoat of his full three-piece suit always rose above the stomach, betraying the feast of *kari-kitchri* he usually enjoyed for lunch.

In 2021 one would describe Khatija as a feminist warrior, a fearless agent of change. Sadly, in 1956 she was just that daughter who ensured that the *kari* never fully digested in Bajee's gut, such was the concern about her future. The prettiest of the sisters, she was also blessed with a witty tongue and devil-may-care attitude. Her ever-obedient sisters would line up at Ma's bed to get their hair oiled and braided with ribbons for school. Khatija, having woken up last, would skilfully negotiate her way to the front of the queue, brushing aside all her sisters' protestations.

The rancid smell of burnt milk would permeate the tiny kitchen when Khatija was on chai-duty. Bajee drank his tea boiled for at least an hour with condensed milk and cardamom. Temperature control was erratic on a coal stove and the daughters worked shifts to ensure that the tea never met the top of the stove. Eventually, Khatija was simply taken off the schedule because cleaning the stove was much more difficult than watching the tea. She was delighted. This confirmed for Ma that she was EXACTLY like Bajee's sisters. Ma did not know what to do with this daughter who shared none of her compliance.

Maverick

Like many men of his time, Bajee was preoccupied with getting his daughters married, one by one, preferably to men who shared his ancestral roots. Many South African people of Indian descent identified quite strongly with the village their forefathers came from. Our family came from a district called Bharuch and people who came from this area were called Kanamias. Strangely, when it was Khatija's turn the universe conspired to find her a suitor who had roots in Bharuch who met with her approval. Even the thought of leaving Fordsburg for Lichtenburg, a small town in the North West Province, did not deter her from the promise of a more independent life than the one she led at home.

Bajee's dream began to materialise. One daughter married to a Kanamia man, one on her way, one to go and Ma had finally given birth to another son several years earlier. The recipes of prayers dictated by his *wali* were paying off and he made a note to purchase a shirt from the Bulbulias in Fietas to thank his religious mentor for his good fortune.

Three months into her marriage, Khatija came back home. She simply knocked on the door of the flat and marched in, suitcase in one hand and appetite for a fight in the other. The honeymoon had ended and she had discovered that she could not live with a pit latrine in Lichtenburg anymore.

"Now you act like you're a millionaire's daughter!" boomed Bajee.

Any daughter, faced with the wrath of her conservative father, would've retreated to the kitchen, to the safety of her mother and sisters. Not Khatija.

She demanded that he allow her to ask for a divorce.

Bajee, convinced that an evil jinn had entered her body, rushed to the Newtown Mosque, *champals* in hand and comb-over hanging limply. Ma too blamed a gene, but one that originated from Bajee's bloodlines.

The maulanas from Newtown Mosque converged on the Vally home offering mediation. They sat in the lounge discussing Khatija's options. She would have none of it. Gate-crashing the tête-à-tête and in fluent Gujarati, she announced to the men that she would not return to her husband and his pit latrine.

Punishment for the divorce came swiftly from all quarters. The Kanamia community in South Africa ostracised my grandparents. Invitations to gatherings were few and far between and women in the community came to "sit" and sympathise. The general consensus was that Ismail Vally's status in the community, despite his forebidding stature, impeccable manners and unequivocal honesty, had slid below the status of the milkman who dropped off two glass bottles of DairyBelle milk every morning in Fordsburg.

Looking back, I prefer to think that Bajee had no choice. Khatija had to be cut loose in order for the family to survive. The Cold War had nothing on the sanctions that were imposed on his tiny brown-paper bag business by the community and Bajee had to strategise in order to salvage his business, his family and his *izzat* – his reputation.

Khatija was asked to leave the family home. Ma knew better than to raise an objection. The only visible difference was that the ever-present wooden *tasbeeh* with a green tassel in her hand moved twice as fast. And her deep blue eyes were always pregnant with tears which threatened to drop their load but never did. This characteristic stayed with Ma until she passed on in 2003.

Dr Rakesh Patel was situated on the corner of Vorster and Malherbe Streets, a block away from the family flat. Khatija, with her characteristic charm, secured herself work as a receptionist for a minimal wage in exchange for being able to sleep on the examination table at night. Her sisters would bring an evening meal, impeccably timed for when Bajee attended *Maghrib* prayers. My mum's recollection of this time is that Khatija, like any revolutionary, simply re-strategised, regrouped and reconsidered her options.

Dissatisfied with taking appointments and embroidering tea cloths in her spare time, she had her sights firmly set on becoming a doctor. Ministerial permission for a young Indian woman to study medicine in South Africa was as likely to be granted as Bajee's blessing for her new venture. No, Khatija would study medicine in Dublin. Many South African boys of Indian heritage were applying and getting accepted. For Khatija, lack of family support, lack of funding and lack of a warm winter jacket to brave the Irish cold were not persuasive enough reasons to stand in her way.

Khatija found funding from the Kholvad House Bursary Fund, which was located in South Africa but carried the name of a village in India. It subsidised her move to Dublin and early years of study. The Kanamia community, satisfied that Bajee had appeased the patriarchy sufficiently by banishing her from the family home, slowly began a reintegration programme. First there were invitations to recitations of the Quran, or *khatams,* and then Ma was asked to join in the washing of meat on a Saturday afternoon for weddings. It was a tiered system and Ma had to work very hard to reach the final stage of acceptance, an invitation to a wedding. Faithful friends who came to "sit" kept Ma updated on the general mood of the community.

Of course, Indian weddings are nothing without a smattering of controversy and so, on one occasion, after the obligatory *duas*, the master of ceremonies thought it appropriate to thank Kholvad House for sponsoring Khatija Vally's ambition to become a doctor. Ma could feel the hours of cleaning chickens and of *khatam*-ing the Quran disappearing into oblivion. Even when Khatija was in the northern hemisphere, she found a way of being among them at the Planet Hotel Hall.

Khatija's only brother-in-law was mortified. "We are not a people who allow people from other villages to educate our people." The irony of the fact that nobody at the wedding had ever set foot in any village in India was lost on him. He graciously undertook to subsidise her studies for the next five years.

Khatija returned to Fordsburg a doctor. Despite Bajee's apparent ambivalence, he was proud enough to summon Ma to cook a pot of biryani, mutton no less, instead of the standard *kari-kitchri*. In trying economic times, this small gesture of pride spoke of forgiveness and remorse and acceptance.

Setting up her practice in Fietas, Khatija gained enormous popularity with the women in the community, often visiting the sick and elderly in their homes and then purchasing the medication from Highbree Pharmacy to hand over in the follow-up visit. Despite her protestations, consultation fees were often settled with a bag of Outspan oranges, crocheted tablecloths or freshly baked coconut biscuits.

Bajee could not have been a prouder father. They would leave together every morning, each with a tiffin. They worked on opposite sides of Fordsburg, he as a street vendor and she as a doctor.

Khatija's grit, determination and ambition paved the way for all her siblings. How was this possible on a street vendor's income? Every working sibling contributed to the education of the other siblings by dropping a portion of their salary into the rusted Mazawattee Tea tin on top of the fridge. Nobody kept *issab-kitaab*. It was a gesture of love and honesty and belief in each other, so there was no need for records and it was always sufficient.

Khatija was modest about her colourful history, insisting that "none of this would have happened, if there were no pit latrines in Lichtenburg".

"If you think about it carefully," she said to me once, "I took the easy way out."

Chapter 8

Ducking Moose

"Mum, don't worry about her. All the teachers say she suffers from ABCD."

My seven-year-old son was trying to empathise with me.

I looked back at the little girl who had approached me a few minutes ago. She had made a beeline for me, ambling casually, and with the grace of a beauty pageant finalist had gingerly stepped on my toes and said to me, "You really should not be late to collect Mikaeel, it's not FAIR!"

Defensively I had snapped my wrist back, glanced at my watch and noticed that I was, in fact, early. This child then ground her foot into my toes as one would extract the last few drops of a lemon impaled on a juicer. Before I could react, she swept her index finger across her throat, smiled guilelessly at me and strode back into the school.

Ducking Moose

I spun my head around, hoping that another parent had witnessed this exchange but everyone seemed distracted, their eyes on the school gates.

After a few minutes, I spotted my boy. He was walking towards me talking to his friends, his hands demonstrating something, no doubt the speed of a racing car. There's something special about watching one's child from afar. We become desensitised to their facial expressions while we're barking instructions in close proximity. It's when they are further away that we can see nuances about their movements and expressions when navigating the world.

"Hey Mum."

"Hey sweetie, am I late?"

"No, why?"

"Well, your friend accosted me just now and basically threatened me and told me not to be late collecting you."

He frowned when I said "accosted". He clearly had no idea what that meant. My tone was desperate, seeking an ally, and he picked up on that.

"It's the ABCD, makes her really annoying." The conviction with which my son said "ABCD" momentarily reversed the roles of adult and child.

Ah, ADHD. Labels everywhere. ODD, ADD, ADHD. Without a doubt, my cousin Shamma would have been diagnosed with oppositional defiance disorder if we had had the language for it at the time. The little girl reminded me of her.

Shamima was a decade older than me to the month. As soon as she could speak, she shortened her name to Shamma, not wanting to use three syllables when two would do.

Often, in utter desperation at my own toddler's temper tantrums, I would phone my Gorimummy and she would say, "No, sorry. Still not as bad as Shamma."

When God handed out personalities, Shamma, having already received the average dose of warmth, humour, sensitivity, anger and passion, kept being shuffled to the back of the queue to receive another dose of these qualities. She held within her so much more than was fair for one human body.

For Gorimummy, Shamma was the equivalent of having triplets.

As a baby, Shamma would cannonball bottles of milk when the temperature was not the perfect degree of lukewarm, something that was difficult to achieve without a microwave. This was invariably followed by loud wailing.

Long before kids were driven to school, when adults too walked to work, the morning routine involved my Gorimummy dragging Shamma, literally pulling and pushing her towards the school, which was 500 metres from the house. Typically, this walk took two minutes, but with Shamma it could take anything up to an hour depending on Shamma's energy levels and Gorimummy's exhaustion. They would arrive at the school bruised, battered and dishevelled.

I always imagine my aunt making a run for it as soon as she deposited her daughter at the classroom. I even imagine her saying, "I got her here, now it's up to you guys," before sprinting the 500 metres back home and bolting the door.

Oo taneh maara – I will hit you.

Today, parents have leverage to bargain, negotiate and reason because there is always a device that our kids want

Ducking Moose

desperately. Psychologists say, "Pick your battles," and we do. Others say, "Hold your ground," and we try. We raise our kids with help from highly educated individuals who dedicate their lives to teaching us how to raise kids who will never need to a sit on a psychologist's couch detailing how our parenting skills got them there.

"*Oo taneh maara*" was all my aunt had in her armour. It was weak, almost laughable. At first the threat was enough to get most of us complying quickly, but not Shamma. Eventually there came a point where the threat seemed empty to all of us and my aunt would overhear us giggling, teasing each other with those words. Gorimummy's now fragile pride meant making good on her threat. Physical punishment was not something that came easily to any adult in the house and it was used sparingly. Simply positioning a hand above the ear and declaring that Bajee was home was often enough of a threat to get all of us flying off in different directions like a startled flock of ducks.

Not Shamma. As soon as the palm of Gorimummy's hand landed on her face, she tried to smack her back, with considerably less restraint. Dramatic pauses were never in her repertoire. Like an athlete throwing the javelin, she put everything she had into it and made it count. So much so, that the dedication and momentum with which she threw the punch propelled her off the chair and into a heap on the floor.

Before long, everyone had learnt not to hit her. She was as fearless as a samurai and not at all intimidated by height and age.

Shamma loved to laugh and she was rarely sad. She would

throw her head back and laugh from a place deep inside her tummy in a way that some people never experience in an entire lifetime. Tears would stream down her face from the laughter. This was a trait she had until her last days.

It was impossible to restrain her once she had decided on a plan of action. A natural leader, she despised school, the House of Delegates curriculum being diametrically opposed to her interests. Some mornings, my aunt would take one look at Shamma's folded arms, her personality threatening to erupt in all its glory at the breakfast table, and concede defeat. Like a gaming character that had just been rebooted, this concession spurred an extraordinary tantrum when it was time for madressa.

Madressa was challenging because, in modern parenting lingo, it was a "non-negotiable" for the kids to attend. Shamma truly believed that attending was a "non-negotiable". She wouldn't go. Maulana Haffeejee, her *ustaad* or teacher, was a neighbour. Having tried corporal punishment and Bajee's stares, both of which failed spectacularly, the family decided that Maulana Haffeejee would come over and reason with her and failing that, pray for her.

It was a meticulously planned sting operation. The doors were locked to stop her from running out of the house. Gorimummy and Bajee were to pin her down in the event of a struggle. Nobody knew exactly what the maulana would do but he was a righteous man, fond of children and very sensible.

He entered the house, greeted everybody warmly, lowered his gaze when he saw the women in the household and asked for a glass of tap water. Shamma tried to make the

Ducking Moose

predicted dash for the street but the ever-open doors were locked. A petulant seven-year-old, she entered the room with the confidence of a boxer entering the ring and sat down opposite him on the couch, never breaking the gaze nor the deadpan expression. Bring it on.

The maulana began quietly reciting the four *Quls*, the prayers for protection, and blowing gently into a glass of water. Everyone watched, waiting to see what he would do next.

And then he made his move. His lips rose in rich Arabic vibrato. He was now reciting *an-Naas*, a prayer called "Mankind". At the same time he dipped his fingers into the water and began splashing droplets onto her face. Instantaneously, Bajee and Gorimummy pinned her shoulders against the couch, hoping that catching every drop of the *pareloo paani* would baptise the insolence out of her. All the time she was kicking her little legs, screeching for him to stop. With Zen-like calmness, he continued reciting verses from the Quran, dipping all five fingers into the water and flicking it into her face.

The water came to an end and her mum and grandfather loosened their grip on her. Everyone thought she would bolt. She didn't. Straightening her shirt and wiping the water off her brow, she brought her head closer to the maulana's head and clearly, unambiguously, said something to him. It rhymes with ducking moose.

The maulana started reading with newfound fervour and dipped his fingers into the glass only to be reminded it was empty. Not to be deterred, he read, in a desperate attempt to master the situation, and, in his desire for the holy words to touch her spirit, he spat. Read and spat. Read and spat. The *surah* lost its melodic quality and was screamed out quickly, punctuated by "TOOH"!

"*Say I seek refuge in the Lord of mankind.*" TOOH!
"*The Sovereign of mankind.*" TOOH!
"*The God of mankind.*" TOOH!
"*From the evil of the sneaking whisperer.*" TOOH!
"*Who whispereth in the hearts of mankind.*" TOOH!
"*Of the jinn and mankind.*" TOOH!

I have heard this story told so many times, both by people who were there and people who weren't there, and none of us get to the end without laughing so hard that each word comes out like a sentence, punctuated by more laughter.

Still. Nobody laughed like Shamma could.

—

"So, you see, potatoes must be cut in discs for chips, not strips. This increases the surface area and then it can hold the maximum amount of vinegar and masala."

I nodded, precariously balancing on a stool that she had positioned below the simmering hot oil.

"The other thing. Throw the discs in all at once and don't stir or touch the pot until they rise. Otherwise you are left with *pap* chips."

Shamma was 15 and I was five. I held on to her every word, having no doubt that I would be quizzed later. That was the thing about her. Nothing was tackled half-heartedly. Being a chubby toddler, I was accustomed to family members pinching my cheeks. Shamma would do that until all the blood had relocated to other parts of my face and then

Ducking Moose

plant wet kisses on the cheeks. She hugged the breath out of me and held on tightly so that when she released me, I would gulp huge amounts of air to compensate for the affection.

She married young, having fallen hopelessly in love, and she would sit on her fiancé's lap and feed him her gourmet disc-shaped chips on Friday nights in full view of the conservative extended family while watching *Noot vir Noot* on TV. Love did not make her placid or demure and she would argue loudly with him about which melody was playing on the game show, convinced she knew it even if the contestants did not.

Shamma was the only sibling in her family not to pursue a tertiary education, but she was an astute businesswoman and had a brilliant understanding of the world of fast-food franchises. Whether it was driving two hours each way, alone, on a Saturday night to purchase cheese for her thriving outlet or jumping in to flip patties if staff members were ill, she threw everything she had at the business. For years after South Africa's democratic elections in 1994 many Indian so-called businessmen havered indecisively about purchasing one of the franchises suddenly available to them. Her franchises were already a phenomenal success.

"Do you ever sleep?" my mum asked her once. That laugh of hers again.

"No Julie *Foi*, what a waste of time!"

The same devotion was lavished on her three sons. Their birthday parties included an amusement park with horses, clowns, magicians – and this was when they could barely walk. The food was prepared by Shamma, these being the days before home industries flourished in Indian communities. She wore the most uncomfortable shoes, always with a pencil heel and bangles to match from wrist to elbow. These multi-coloured plastic bangles would collapse in exhaustion at the end of the day. All day, they worked their way from wrist to elbow, backwards and forwards. Whether it was to boil a kettle or light candles on the birthday cake, Shamma ran. There was an urgency about every moment of her life which was difficult to understand.

The youngest of her sons was barely three months old when she was diagnosed with lupus. This chronic disease occurs when the immune system becomes hyperactive and attacks healthy tissue. Shamma had the most severe form and having a stroke was a real threat. "Slow down, bed rest, don't stress." The advice, for Shamma, was a death threat in itself.

At 32 she did suffer a massive stroke which left her bedridden, with little movement in the arms. By the time we all visited her in bed, barely able to digest the bleak prognosis, Shamma was five steps ahead, proclaiming that this was a minor setback and that she expected to walk within three months. I don't doubt that she believed that this was possible.

The loss of her ability to speak was heartbreaking. It was weeks before those close to her could make sense of what she needed to say. The rest of us would chatter like monkeys and update her on our lives hoping that she would not ask a question or make a comment which we did not understand. Silly us. She would ask many questions and we would look at each other, not understanding, and her frustration would grow more intense.

Ducking Moose

Sometimes, if the story was funny, the tears would roll down her eyes in silent laughter. We spoke in hyperbole to lighten the atmosphere but soon realised that it was we, not she, that needed that inspiration. She was *compos mentis* and would sometimes roll her eyes or look away if she thought that a guest was being pitying.

She hardly watched TV but kept abreast of the news and loved for one of us to visit and discuss it with her. The expression on her face would play its part in a fruitful discussion. She'd purse her lips in disgust at the latest corruption scandal or smile if we shared good news with her.

There are so many things about Shamma that I will never forget. Perhaps it was the way she said "I'm very well" every single time we asked how she was. It is also how she never, not once, asked "Why me?" Self-pity was not a part of her psyche. For years, she pursued every available option there was in her determination to walk again, from gimmicky magnetic pulses to a trip to an ashram in India.

The lupus continued to ravage her body, despite large amounts of cortisone. Gorimummy and Elsie, the care worker, bathed her daily and fed her tiny morsels patiently, as one would a new baby. In 14 years, Shamma didn't develop a single bedsore, testament to the skill of Elsie and Gorimummy, who were always at her side.

In an act of complete selflessness, she gave custody of her three sons to her ex-husband, to raise with his new wife. She never called them by their names without adding the word "my" as a title. All mothers love their sons but they were her *beloved* sons.

The disease grew progressively worse over the years and

there were several dalliances with death. Any terminal illness, in particular one that is so debilitating, has an effect on the mind of the sufferer. With God having given Shamma so much personality and a sound mind up until her last day, as family, we often wished for her to be less aware, less clear and less lucid.

"We have lost Shamma." My dad called me late one Friday afternoon. Relief. The same relief I would feel when, as a toddler, she would loosen her grip on me after a rib-crunching hug.

Her funeral, for want of a better word, was festive. After the extended family had left, we sat down in Gorimummy's kitchen and reminisced about the force that was our cousin. We drank tea, we dunked cake and, given half a chance, would've hosted a wake. We cried for the life she could have had. We remembered how she drank life in huge breathless gulps. And, of course, we remembered the ducking moose, only this time we were all old enough to say it like she did.

Chapter 9

Enough is as Good as a Feast

There are 25 ingredients in the recipe for Baklava Cheesecake. Preparation time: 17 hours, 30 minutes.

"Does it have to be a Baklava Cheesecake?" my husband asked, looking at the picture of the pulled sugar topping and having serious doubts about my ability. "How about a trifle?"

I laughed and gave him three reasons why a trifle would not be appropriate for Eid.

Lazy people make trifle.

Stingy people make trifle.

An Eid dessert must have a double-barrelled name. I could make Turkish Delight *Soji*, Cinnabon Pudding or Baklava Cheesecake.

Trifle failed on all three counts. It was an old-fashioned

dessert, not worth Instagramming. I started to reflect on how much had changed from the Eids of my childhood.

Perhaps the greatest culinary transition from the 1980s to the new millennium is the Eid salad.

Salad in 1980 involved digging deep into the wooden crater at the local greengrocer for an iceberg lettuce with bright green leaves, one that would befit an Eid table. The outer leaves were discarded, the balance wrapped tightly like an Egyptian mummy and then cut into party streamers. Carrots were simply grated and formed the inner concentric circle of a platter covered with delicate hand-painted flowers. A juicy tomato was quartered and then quartered again and placed randomly on the lettuce and carrots. As this was an Eid salad, the woman of the house would splurge on radish and these would sit like water lilies on the pond of vegetation. Salt and lemon juice would rain down on the salad in a final flourish as the dishing-out spoon hit the base of the biryani pot and the matriarch declared that it was steamed to perfection.

When it comes to biryani, aroma is everything and my *daadi*, my paternal grandmother, is fabled to have been able to judge whether or not salt was lacking simply by the smell of the vapour. Never, never and never again will my mum Julie tentatively dip a dessert spoon in halfway through the cooking process, as she was once loudly accused of doing, ruining the Mughal dish half-way through by allowing steam to escape, and with it, the flavour of royalty.

By the late 1980s, most Indian women invested in a wavy cutter, as the simplicity of a knife would no longer do and

Enough is as Good as a Feast

the carrots for the salad were subjected to all sorts of artistic ambitions. Mostly the carrots resembled Willards chips but some artists got carried away and rivalled Salvador Dali with abstract placements of the vegetables, culminating in surrealist flying carrots and winged olives. The salads were assembled on ostensibly white dishes, but these were merely a canvas and many domestic helpers went home in December with platters covered with hand-painted flowers. At about the same time feta, olives and cherry tomatoes were discovered and store-bought Greek salad dressing became a staple condiment to complement the salad. The demand for radish dropped so dramatically that the greengrocer stopped stocking the sharp garnish.

Even nowadays, the younger females in extended families are usually asked to prepare the Eid salad, the biryani not yet entrusted to their inexperienced hands. The salad is usually built up in layers. The bottom is often an explosion of colour including every species in the lettuce family, stringed carrots and Roma tomatoes. That base is covered with the feta, olives and halved cucumber that form the middle layer. In a show of economic stability, the top layer now includes pomegranate seeds, gooseberries, strawberries and avocado. Why stop at vegetables? Khala-next-door would balk at the expensive *badaam* deep-fried in oil, olive oil no less, and sprinkled liberally on the pinnacle.

There was a time when I felt that much of the joy had been sucked out of Eid. As hard as I tried, I could not invoke the spirit of my childhood Eid. Nor could I replicate the joy for my sons. They had lost sight of the simplicity of the celebration and I felt partly responsible. There was no indication in my home that Eid was soon, there was simply no Eid atmosphere. Shouting over the PlayStation, one day my son said to me, "I really don't care what I wear for Eid, anything will do." I was gutted.

As a child, we were spoilt for choice between the four shops that serviced two provinces for Eid clothes in the Oriental Plaza. If you didn't find your special outfit at Minty's, Abram Stores, Pick 'n Wear or Docrat's, you would not be celebrating Eid. Families from smaller towns piled into cars during the fasting month, hoping to make it back home before sunset but preparing a stash of samoosas just in case. The smell would assault the nostrils of the fasting children, but the suffering paled in comparison to the prospect of new Eid clothes from the city with a skyline.

The Price Mecca was a stone's throw from Newtown and my mother Julie would be deployed to source the girl cousins' Eid clothes from Minty's every year. It was in 1985 that she flouted the brief and discarded the ridiculously long list with all her nieces' names, ages, colour preferences and specific instructions. She found one outfit, played it safe by choosing it in white and read out different sizes to the sales assistant. Looking back, the one-piece cat suit with red embroidery on the shoulders, a tasselled red rope belt and elasticated wrists and ankles was ridiculous. The sleeves opened like a butterfly with a loose white drape from shoulder to wrist. All things considered, we looked like the Indian version of The Supremes.

She sold it to all of us. Look! Match-match! It was new, it was Eid and no adult was going to entertain any complaints from the nieces when there were carrots to grate and chickens to be feathered and cut and washed. We lined up, all eight of us, aged between five and 16, taking photos with the Kodak camera and arranging ourselves into all sorts of configurations, massive smiles, holding our arms out to show off the design of the outfit to its full effect. Those photos never fail to reduce my sullen teenage son into fits of laughter followed by threats to leak the black-bordered prints onto the Internet.

The job of trawling the malls for Eid clothes for my sons has fallen to my husband, Yusuf. Knowing that it was her first born who had chosen a Zam-Buk T-shirt for his son's first Eid and a Lucky Star Pilchards T-shirt for his second made explaining things to my mother-in-law less awkward. The third Eid was marginally better: my son was encouraged to voice his preference so he wore Ben 10 pyjamas to Eid lunch and Yusuf was impressed that the shorts were free.

Having no daughter, I almost forgot that the magic of *mehndi* had been inextricably linked to the joy of Eid for me. Scrubbed and squeaky clean in our Eid pyjamas with our damp hair smelling like gardenia on a spring morning, we would converge on Ma's house. (Being so close to Newtown Mosque, we were always one of the first families to get the news that the moon had been sighted.) One of the aunts would produce several square bank bags that held the *mehndi*. We would take turns, my cousins and I, sniffing the earthy heady scent, wondering which packet held the promise of the deep saffron colour we were hoping to achieve. Debate would rage about whether using lemon juice or coffee as a catalyst would help us achieve the result we wanted. We settled on lemon juice as the mixing agent after Gorimummy let drop that a Pakistani woman whom we all knew did bridal *mehndi* used lemon juice. A chipped saucer, toothpicks and Sellotape completed the tools and we would wait for an adult to blend the mixture over a steel basin. The eldest female cousin would be tasked with overseeing younger clumsy hands and we would be ushered out of the kitchen to create space for the older women in the house to start preparing the biryani.

In the 1980s, long before Tim Noakes promulgated his gospel of full-fat dairy, ghee was considered certain to send us all to an early grave. My uncle, by now an ob-gyn, would keep a close eye on the generosity with which his sisters used the poison. He would turn away for a second and another massive spoonful would be ladled into the biryani. Of course, they would nod in endorsement of his expertise and agree with him wholeheartedly the following day about how delicious ghee-less biryani actually could be. There would have been at least two pounds of the liquid gold in that pot.

While my mum and her sisters took turns distracting their brother from the ghee, my cousins and I would sit on a large, old sheet in the lounge decorating each other's hands. There was a year when I was seven and my cousin Tashmia, who was 11, was my hero. I trusted her when she insisted that daisies were outdated and that geometric shapes were in vogue. Having been introduced to geometry in Standard 5, she artfully designed three triangles on my hand: equilateral, isosceles and acute, proudly exclaiming that my design was cutting edge. We passed around a sliced lemon, squeezing it over the drying *mehndi*, coaxing the colour along.

Enough is as Good as a Feast

Like all things when we were growing up, patience was taught to us by the limitations of how things worked. Nothing was instant; the best results were achieved by waiting. Richness of colour was directly proportionate to the waiting time and so our *mehndi* was a very public display of the patience of the wearer.

Clearly, that was a virtue I had developed. I fought my mum to leave my hand alone as she attempted to wash the *mehndi* off before she tucked me into bed. Mother knows best. Having fallen asleep with my hand under my cheek, I wore a rich, deep orange geometric pattern on my face for six weeks after Eid. How I wished that I had insisted on a daisy instead.

Now we outsource this important ritual. These days I rush into Eastern Temptations to purchase a packet of sliced almonds for the salad I have been commissioned to harvest for Eid. Nobody can be bothered to mix powdered *mehndi* when it is now factory produced, available mixed and in a tube. I watch the 30 young girls all with a R50 note in one hand and a smartphone in the other queuing impatiently to slap their hand down on a plastic table and, in five minutes flat, walk away with a hand befitting a bride. There is such irony in the mandala precision of the patterns being churned out on the conveyor belt of impatience. The designs are spectacular but the patrons always seem underwhelmed and who can blame them? A box has been ticked. The quick-drying *mehndi* will be washed off their hands as soon as they reach home, in a celebration of instant gratification.

I am told that before I was born the chickens for Eid

biryani were purchased by Bajee on his way home from work and carried home alive, hung upside down, feet tied. They would be exhausted by the time they arrived. After his chai he would call his youngest son, Rasid-Ahmed, to assist him in the slaughter, plucking and dismemberment of the birds. Rasid-Ahmed would hesitantly walk into the outdoor bathroom as though it was the first time he had seen a chicken. His demeanour, coupled with the chicken's tantrum, would have Bajee sweating profusely and secretly thinking that one of his daughters would be more competent. Rasid-Ahmed's hatred of the act was always intensified by his sisters' gloating.

My mum and her sisters would stand behind the closed door, listening closely to the fracas inside and repeating Bajee's annoyed mutterings to each other. They loved their younger brother but relished the awkwardness with which he approached this task. It was the ONE thing he had to do, compared to the thousand things his sisters did, but he would have happily cooked, managed the laundry load, scrubbed floors and washed windows every day for years to avoid being in that outdoor bathroom with his father. As far as Bajee was concerned, it was a great honour. Rasid-Ahmed would hold the chicken at arm's length and try to look away over his shoulder until the bird stopped struggling and was declared halaal, his face screwed into a knot at the bird's agony. Feathers would fly and the bird would cluck its last.

I'm told that the next steps are akin to a gory massacre. I wouldn't know because my chickens arrive at my house dead, washed, bloodless, frozen and packaged on a polystyrene tray in a classic nine-piece configuration.

Enough is as Good as a Feast

Things were different when Rasid-Ahmed, the darling of the family, left to study medicine at UCT and returned for Eid the following year. He readily jumped up to assist Bajee in the slaughter of the chickens and even volunteered to get an early start while Bajee was drinking his chai. That year, the chicken hardly put up a fight and Bajee looked at his son with elation, thinking that one year at medical school had given his son the hands of a surgeon.

Rasid-Ahmed was named by his father. The woman at Home Affairs, bored by the monotony of her job and unaffected by the importance of this child arriving after five daughters, asked my grandfather for his name.

"Ismail," he said, and in that way, carelessly or rather uncaringly, gave Rasid-Ahmed his father's first name as a surname.

She was also too comfortable in her presumed superiority to bother checking the spelling of his first name and what was meant to be Rashid-Ahmed was written as Rasid-Ahmed. He is the only one of Bajee's children not to have the surname Vally.

The Minister who granted him permission to study medicine at UCT didn't care either, but his friends, knowing the family well, nicknamed him "Wally".

One would think that the adoration with which he was raised, coupled with being an ob-gyn in an Indian community to whom doctors are demi-gods, would turn him into a spoilt brat. But he remains one of the kindest, most mindful and unaffected men I know. Until Ma's death, he would dish a plate of *kari-kitchri* for the two of them, take it her bedroom and share it with two forks, neither of them actually hungry but revelling in the closeness of the ritual.

The year he returned for Eid from Cape Town, extra saffron was infused in the biryani and Ma's hands were liberal in using all her ingredients *ahre ahre* – without measurement. Her son was home for Eid and judging by Bajee's jovial mood, the chicken preparation had gone well; her son was a man. That is perhaps why she was the only one who refused to believe that he had used chloroform, which he had appropriated from medical school, to subdue the energetic chicken, which was the reason the biryani tasted like a cadaver.

Although there was no mistaking the heavy odour of the laboratory liquid, Ma blamed the *adoo masala* in the biryani. The tubs of *adoo masala* got thrown out that year and, knowing what a fresh batch would involve, my mum's heart broke. Still, everyone shielded Rasid-Ahmed from any accusations.

Adoo masala is a ground paste made of blended dry red chillies, ginger and garlic which forms the base of most Indian cooking. Usually, enough was made to be handed out to daughters-in-law, daughters, cousins and those who claimed that "nobody makes it as nicely as you do". For a week before making it, during ginger season, my mum would frequent the vegetable vendors, usually Jaara Raman at Rama's, Hamid's in the Plaza and Dharee Wara's or Akoojee's on Bree Street, now Lillian Ngoyi Street. Every day she would report to Ma on the quality, freshness and price. Because she lived in the area, she would get tip-offs about when the freshest deliveries would be arriving. The vendors always promised to keep aside a "nice box" and then they would randomly grab the first box on the top of the pile when she arrived to collect. Still, the pedantic devotion to the rituals involved in the preparation of *adoo masala* would put ancient civilisations to shame.

Once the ginger had been purchased (somehow Akoojee's always won the tender), the box would lie threateningly on top of the box freezer. The massive task had to be tackled soon, while the ginger was fat and juicy with flavour and before mould rendered it useless. The ginger would first have to be scraped naked of its skin, then laid in a *skottel* like arthritic bones. Ma was the forewoman, the quality control, and she would retrieve pieces and throw them right back into a daughter's pile if they were not scraped perfectly. The pieces were then blended to a paste in a rudimentary steel mincer attached to the edge of the kitchen table. Handfuls of all three ingredients would be dropped into a hole the size of a yo-yo while another participant turned the handle clockwise to grind the blend.

The process would start with the younger children begging for an opportunity to turn the handle. Experience taught Ma to concede because after half an hour the queue to grind would have disappeared. The machine would often get stuck, a stubborn piece of ginger refusing to accept its fate. Then the cook would have to reverse the handle and grind counter-clockwise until the culprit surfaced, was cut with a knife and then thrown back to meet its inevitable kismet. Some pieces were so stubborn that feet would rise off the floor and the grinder's entire body weight would be thrown into decimating the root.

There were always complaints from the women about

how fibrous this season's ginger was, how dull the chillies looked and how small the garlic segments were. Next year, a new vendor must be supported. Aunty Salma's *adoo masala* came out *mashallah* and we should find out where she buys from. These were all calculated complaints, a point of reference if for any reason the final product did not live up to the previous year's high standard. The complaints also protected the final product from any clumsy hands and evil eyes and they were all careful not to praise the *adoo masala* until the last teaspoon had been decanted into the last margarine tub. Suddenly, "one thing", you can't beat Akoojee's ginger and "Did you see how red-red the chillies were?" Relief. And Akoojee's produce would be returned to the pedestal which it (still) richly deserves.

The first batch of the *adoo masala* in The Chloroform Year was particularly perfect.

This year I took a bow at Eid lunch. I was tempted to rename the dessert to sound exotic and glamorous but trifle it was and I served it with pride and replaced the peaches with strawberries. The double- and triple-barrelled desserts sulked and balked at the demise of the trifle, as did their creators. My uncle, scraping the base of the dish, commented that the dessert was a "classic", one that took him back to Eids gone by, and I was glad that I had chosen to celebrate the family instead of the food.

Chapter 10

Julian

I was bullied into taking the biryani to my late aunt's husband. It was Eid and she had been gone for nine months. My mum has special access to my self-chastising conscience and looked pleadingly at me when the kitchen cleared as she was packing the food into an empty 2-litre DairyBelle ice-cream tub. My sister has the ability to disappear without much fanfare and I stood in the kitchen desperately hoping that I could think of an excuse.

"It's so much *sawab* if you do this for them." And when it did not look like I was being moved by the promise of heavenly rewards, "Do this for Zunaid, your aunt would've appreciated it."

A deep sigh as I wedged the *dhai* between the handbrake and seat.

"Remember Uncle Anwar is a bit deaf so hoot loudly and keep hooting until he comes out."

I drove to the part of Mayfair that is known as Little Mogadishu, navigating between Opel Astras driving on either side of me. Breaking into a light sweat, I slowed down as I contemplated the rule "keep left, pass right". It was disorientating and I cursed loudly as cars sped past on either side of me. Nervously, I gripped the steering wheel tightly and my fingernails were white and my hands stiff as I got out of the car.

Zunaid was sitting in the sun on the lowest of three concrete steps, smoking a cigarette.

"Hey Zunaid, *Eid Mubarak* ... Is your dad here? Brought you guys some biryani."

Zunaid looked at me and pointed down the concrete passage. I was disappointed that he did not smile: the dimple in his right cheek peeked through the beard but he would have to smile for me to see it in all its magnificent charm. That dimple was so deep that usually when he spoke it would play hide and seek with me.

Just then Uncle Anwar popped his head out of the front door and said, "Raznoo!"

I had to smile. He is the only person in the world who calls me that. He adds that double "o" to all our names.

"Come inside, I have to show you photos of how nice I fixed up your aunty's *kabr* with flowers and new plants for Eid." He patted both the pockets of his trousers hoping to find his cell phone. It was not there. "Wait, I can just sketch the layout for you."

"I would love to, but I have to take my kids somewhere ... show my mum, she will be happy to see." I have lost count of the number of times I have used my children as an excuse. In Uncle Anwar's head, they are probably still toddlers.

"You young girls always in a hurry, just like my Ansoo and Shamoo."

I waved to him through my open window. I was 44 years old and his daughters were older than me, but the compliment made me smile. I knew, with the same certainty that I know that the sun will rise tomorrow, that if I stopped moving at any point from the time he laid eyes on me until the time I closed my car door, I would enter a black hole. No rattling of car keys, no emergency, would enable me to disengage from conversation with Uncle Anwar. He drew one in and hours later, mouth dry and feet aching, there was still no polite way of disengaging. Usually he started with "Can I ask you just one question?"

The "one question" that I once got when I was 17 was, "What is this internet thing?" I did not have kids at the time and I was not as good as I am now at sourcing excuses, so he listened to me for hours, enchanted by the possibilities of the World Wide Web. He brought out an old A4 book and drew as I spoke and even though nothing he was drawing was making sense to me, I was flattered that my layperson's explanation was creating a blueprint in his head. Skype meant that he and my aunt could see and chat to their daughters in New York. Forgetting myself in his excitement, I promised to accompany him to Makro to purchase a laptop and we examined everything on offer for hours only to be told that he thought that the set-up cost would be in the region of R200, not R20 000, but it was lovely spending time with me.

Uncle Anwar was married to one of my aunts. Both doctors, they had opened a surgery in a small mining town in Mpumalanga called Kinross and secured a contract with a local mine to treat all its employees. They were the only doctors in the small town and the queue to consult with them would start at 5am. By 7am when the doors opened the trickle of sickly miners would have grown to a queue 500 metres long. The doctors slogged, often switching the lights off only at 9pm. The receptionist would walk down the long queue at 6pm and declare a cut-off point. As soon as she left, more miners would join the queue and my aunt often did not have the heart to turn anybody away. The shuttle service from the hostel to their surgery would stop running at 7pm and that was the only way to guarantee that the conveyor belt of patients would wind down. All of Uncle Anwar's patients would leave with a script in one hand and a pencil sketch of what was wrong with them in the other. The surgery had a long corridor with single beds and curtains and a small trolley of doctors' equipment in each cubicle. It looked very much like a fitting room in a chain store without the mirrors. Watching them work was exhausting. Every 15 minutes curtains would be opened and drawn and a new patient would lie down, waiting his turn.

Their three children, a son and two daughters, spent weekends playing in the open veld opposite their home. We would sometimes visit and Zunaid would bring out special cardboard for me to slide down a grassy embankment. He had built a go-kart and we would take turns zooming down the gravel road. He was 12 and there were a number of structural issues with his design – the tyres were held

Julian

together with wire and would unravel and he never got to adding a steering device – so one of us would invariably fall off. We would all walk home behind the injured cousin, who would be limping and nursing the raw scrape to the knee.

Standard practice called for red Mercurochrome to be dunked in cotton wool and patted liberally on all open wounds. This would often make one look even worse for wear. You got two types of families: the Mercurochrome kind or the gentian violet kind; nobody straddled the line when it came to antiseptic. If, by chance, I or my sister was injured near a friend's house and that family used a different antiseptic, Mum would say "What is that?" instead of "What happened to you?" and we would feel a deep betrayal. By the end of primary school, allegiance to one or the other had been established for the next generation. The choice of Zam-Buk or Germolene held the same fierce competitiveness. My mum would sniff the air and ask, "What is that smell?" Again, I had cheated on the family's value system.

Zunaid was the eldest of the crew, then came my sister, then his sisters and then me. We would make-believe that we were the Famous Five and yes, I had made peace with being Timothy the dog. It was a silent part mostly, but I struggled to keep up with them, so I was just happy that they allowed me to tag along. It was that magical age between toddlerhood and adolescence when children can be left to play unsupervised, and a minor accident usually brought everyone back home. Those were the years of toe-jam and unwashed hair and knee grazes. Zunaid's bedroom had sketches of the design of the go-kart he kept improving on. Weeks would pass between the last knee-scrape and our next visit and if the scab had healed, the trust would return. Like Leonardo da Vinci, he added arrows and explanations and worked very hard to engineer a fail-safe go-kart. But I think that Newton's laws were only taught in Standard 6. If someone had explained that every object will remain in uniform motion in a straight line unless compelled to change its state by the action of an external force, we would have known that a bend in the road without a steering or breaking feature would not end well.

Kinross was a six-square-kilometre town without a high school. Zunaid had turned 12 and my aunt and uncle had made the difficult decision to send him to an elite boarding school in Woodmead, in Johannesburg's northern suburbs. A gifted learner, he was promoted to Standard 8 after the first term at the new school. Being 12, away from home for the first time, culturally lost and forced to socialise with much older children, Zunaid did whatever he could to fit in. He was introduced to drugs and alcohol at 13 and by the time his parents understood the magnitude of the addiction, he was eight months away from matric exams. Uncle Anwar sold his surgery in Kinross, purchased a flat in Fordsburg, relocated his family to Mayfair and set out to get Zunaid accepted into Medicine at Wits University. All of this in eight months. He turned the flat in Fordsburg into a study centre for himself and Zunaid. For weeks he locked his son in the flat to ensure that he had no access to drugs and alcohol. My aunt pleaded to be able to see her son, but Uncle Anwar was adamant.

"It is not a pretty sight," he would say, "but it is necessary."

After a two-month detox, father and son began preparing for matric exams. Each room was focused on a different subject, with large chart paper and flow diagrams. They worked frantically through maths past papers, often racing each other for speed and accuracy. Food was brought to the flat and all contact with the outside world was suspended. Uncle Anwar drove to Pretoria to purchase past papers and was only satisfied that Zunaid was adequately prepared when he completed the past papers from the previous ten years and managed to achieve 90% in each paper. If Zunaid did not make that mark, Uncle Anwar would give the paper back to him and ask him to "find" the missing marks.

Zunaid walked into Medicine at Wits the following year.

Campus parties were synonymous with beer and cheap wine in cardboard containers and it was during the preparation for the annual rag that alcohol proved irresistible. One night, after a residence party, he slammed his olive-green Honda into a solid wall as the road curved. He was drunk, he used the brakes too late, the car was too fast and the steering wheel buckled under his chest.

Doctors at Baragwanath Hospital attached weights to his head and hoped for the best, inducing a coma. They knew that the meaning of the dispassionate medical explanations of the state of Zunaid's brain injury was not lost on his medically qualified parents. Uncle Anwar stood at his son's bed, sketchbook ready, waiting for a neurologist to walk past, and, as the neurologist spoke, he would sketch a medical explanation of what was being said to him. In the hours between the doctors' visits, both he and my aunt would read to Zunaid. Piles of *Reader's Digest*s were stored under his stretcher and they would tick off the ones they had read to him. Eight months later, just as his mum finished "Here come the VCRs" and started "Time bomb in our tap water", Zunaid stirred.

They brought their son home nine months after the accident. Initially he was quiet, thoughtful and reclusive. But the relief of having Zunaid home muted what turned out to be alarm bells.

"There is radioactive DNA in the tap water, don't drink it!" Zunaid pushed aside his mum's hand violently. The glass she was holding to her lips smashed against the tiles. Her explanation was that all those *Reader's Digest* articles got muddled in his head while he was comatose and he was having difficulty adjusting to being *compos mentis*.

He would watch hours of television series like *Night Court* and *Moonlighting* while snacking on Flanagan's green onion crisps with Tropika. They were just grateful for his life and ignored the sniggers they heard from him when he was alone and the deadpan expressions he wore in company.

But when Zunaid lifted a kitchen knife and charged at his 13-year-old sister to protect her from the alien in the VCR, they visited a psychiatrist.

The psychiatrist went through the symptoms of schizophrenia, almost all of which Zunaid presented with. It is characterised by aggression, agitation, depression, anger, fear, hallucination, paranoia, fatigue, delusion, disorientation, hearing voices, inactivity, hyperactivity, apathy, memory loss and mental confusion. The severity of Zunaid's illness meant that it was not uncommon for him to experience all the symptoms in one day.

The sketchbook lay limply on Uncle Anwar's lap and

eventually slid off and landed on the floor. There was nothing to sketch.

Was it the alcohol and drug abuse in his early years? Maybe.

Was it the environment at boarding school? Perhaps.

Was it the pressure of the preparation for matric exams? Possibly.

Was it the head injury? Conceivably.

Was it the genetic link to his grandfather, who had a mental illness? Very likely.

Did any of this matter?

Can a family suffer a death without anybody dying? It was a painful choice, daily, between forcing him to take the sedating medication and living with a violent child. He would beg my aunt not to make him take the medication, which reduced him to a compliant zombie. She would sometimes insist and then she and Uncle Anwar would have to physically restrain him to get it down. My aunt was petite: some of these struggles left her with bruised wrists and she was often thrown clean across the room by her 20-year-old son. Grinding the medication into his food rarely worked because Zunaid would go on a hunger strike.

The impact of not taking the medication was worse. They gave up on having a TV after he smashed the third one. His sisters tiptoed around the house, ducking behind furniture if he entered a room, often taking all their meals in their bedrooms and locking the door to escape his violence.

On days when his parents managed to get the medication down, my aunt would look at him with tears streaming down her face. He became an expressionless piece of chain-smoking furniture. Curtains were drawn during daylight hours as having them open seemed to exacerbate the paranoia. My uncle and aunt worked shifts all day and night making sure that he did not self-harm or take one of their lives. He would wake up throughout the night and pace. Any locked door aggravated his paranoia and he would bang incessantly and get increasingly agitated if his sisters did not open up. To allow them to have a restful night's sleep, one parent would stay awake and try to coax Zunaid back to bed before he discovered a locked door.

Why not just medicate the hell out of him? Because they remembered their son. They remembered the Pink Floyd fan who would work at his table for hours on a go-kart design. The boy whose dimples threatened to swallow his face when he was told that he was intellectually gifted and could be anything he wanted to be, even an engineer. The boy who was so good-looking that the fact that he did not know this made him all the more attractive. The boy whose dry sense of humour had us all pulling faces at his lame, but witty, jokes. The voracious reader whose books filled more bags than clothes when they took him to boarding school. The child who was Julian, the leader of the Famous Five. My aunt remembered until the day she died.

Zunaid's illness made the surgery in Kinross feel like something that happened a lifetime ago.

Uncle Anwar was dabbling in the property market when I had just started my first year at Wits. Before caller ID, one simply answered a phone that rang, not thinking about the rabbit's hole that one could enter on answering.

"Raznoo! I'm so glad I got you. Your mummy tells me you

are working very hard at Wits!"

Hours of sitting on the floor at Solomon Mahlangu House sipping stale coffee flashed by.

"Yes, Uncle Anwar. How can I help you?"

"Well, you know I have bought a number of houses in Mayfair and I'm turning them into student accommodation but I'm not sure what to put in each room."

"*Ja* ... so ..."

"So, I need you to come with me to a res room at Wits ... I need your student card for access and then we won't be long."

"THEN WE WON'T BE LONG?!"

By now my mother was looking at me, thinking that I needed all the *sawab* I could get, and I just said "yes". Just. Like. That.

He picked me up at 7pm and I spent the short drive telling him how I only had 20 minutes to spare because I had an assignment due the next day. I did not have children, so my excuses were feeble.

We entered the residence. I remember looking at him, thinking, *How do we do this? Knock on a door, ask for someone else and he quickly peeks into the room?*

He was ahead of me and stopped and knocked.

Please don't open.

A young girl, she must have been a first- or second-year student, opened the door a crack and Uncle Anwar just jumped into it. He introduced himself to her, asked if we could come in, and then shoved me to the front to legitimise his story. "This is Raznoo."

Sheepishly, I confirmed his story and she graciously let

us in and answered questions about the desk, the bed, the cupboards and the meals at residences. We were ready to leave – in fact, I had made it out of the door – when something caught Uncle Anwar's eye.

Anatomy of the Ear.

"So Krish, can I call you Krishnoo ... You studying medicine?"

"Yes."

"Do you understand this section?"

"Sort of."

"Can I have 20 minutes of your time?"

"Ummmm ..."

"Do you have a sketch pad?"

"Ummmm ..."

"Never mind, here it is."

I do not know if it was because we were from the same cultural grouping, or if it was by then clear that we were not going to kill her, or she genuinely needed help with the anatomy of the ear, but what I witnessed next was the most poignant thing I have ever seen.

Krish sat down next to him. Uncle Anwar cleared his throat and by the time he was done, I could easily have written an exam on the anatomy of the ear. He drew, he followed up with clear explanations, he cross-referenced with the textbook, he threw in anecdotes about the design of the ear, he marvelled at the genius of God in conceptualising the ear.

The tutorial was magnificent. Krish, whoever she was, looked enraptured by Uncle Anwar's passion. She had no idea how much those 30 minutes meant to the man. She had no context for what was unfolding but all I could see in my head were images of Zunaid and I knew how desperately Uncle Anwar needed her to excel in this exam.

"So Krishnoo, from one colleague to another, all the best. I promise that you will never struggle with the anatomy of the ear again."

In that moment, I had no doubt that she would become an ENT specialist.

My aunt passed away in January 2019. She was 83. For 34 long years she and Uncle Anwar lived with Zunaid and managed the mental illness. One of them stayed awake while he slept. It was inconceivable for either parent to consider admitting him to a care home for people with mental illness. "He is my son," she would say, as though that fact would change the absurd suggestion. We saw glimpses of the Zunaid that we knew but they were infrequent. He would lie on his back in his bedroom for hours, blowing smoke rings, and I would wonder how, with so much going on in his head, he could do so little with his time. Recently Riaz, a cousin from Cape Town, visited Zunaid a month before Eid and asked if there was anything he could get him. Music, some books, "Didn't you enjoy listening to Pink Floyd?"

Largely Zunaid would ignore us when we spoke but this time, alert as a meerkat, he smiled at Riaz and with his characteristic dry sense of humour, dimples in full bloom, he said, "A car, you could buy me a car."

Chapter 11

Red Riding Hood

My mother's younger brother Rasid-Ahmed was a cry baby. If her timing was perfect, she could grab the pink dummy from his mouth, suck the life out of it and return it to his sullen mouth before his whining reached her mother's ears. Ma, my grandmother, would have to heat castor oil daily to pour into his ears to ease the chronic ear infection he seemed to have been born with. Really, my mother thought to herself, all this fuss for a boy-child and when he does arrive, his ears are faulty.

My mother Julie and her brother, 18 months her junior, were stuck as playmates. All their siblings were at school.

"Want to play marbles, Julie?"

"Only if I can have my dummy back for five minutes."

He held out the dummy willingly with the impish grin

that he still has, one hand behind his back and his head cocked to one side.

Just as my mother was about to seal the deal, Bajee, my grandfather, walked into the room and Rasid-Ahmed shoved the dummy right back into his mouth. He started humming in mock innocence. It had been decided that my mother, being five years old, was too old for a dummy but Rasid-Ahmed, being slightly younger, was just the right age. It seemed a poor return on investment for my grandparents to purchase a new dummy for the new baby when there was one available, so my mother's dummy was abruptly ripped from her mouth. No weaning, no pacifying. Gone.

Bajee looked at his two youngest children and asked, "Who wants to come with me to Uncle Manhattan?"

Just then, Ma entered the room and told Bajee softly, in Gujarati, to leave Rasid-Ahmed at home. The August wind was strong and she had just poured castor oil in his ears and the wind would "catch" them.

"Julie?" my mother's breath quickened and she nodded eagerly before Bajee could say "*Jaldi*". All his requests were followed by the word *jaldi*. He would have his tea *jaldi*, he was ready to leave for work and would need his tiffin *jaldi*.

This hulk of a man, my grandfather, raised his arm ever so slightly to signal to my mother that she could hold his hand. Her arm had to be practically vertical to hold Bajee's hand and like this, they set off.

The irony of Bajee's suits needing to be dry-cleaned at Manhattan Dry Cleaners when Ma subsidised the family's income by hand-washing piles of laundry for the wealthy Afrikaans families in Fietas is not lost on me. But a man deserves one luxury and his was getting his three-piece suits professionally steamed.

My mother's arm raised above her head to reach her father's hand, with a stupid grin, father and daughter braved the wind and set off slowly towards Manhattan Dry Cleaners. The walk took them down Jenning Street and into Bree street, past Akoojee's Fruit and Vegetable shop, the material shop on the corner and Rama's Fruiterers. Paunchy Jaara Raman sat on his little uncomfortable three-legged stool on the intersection between Bree and Jennings Streets. Bajee touched his fedora hat in greeting.

If Bajee was a man of few words, the *cha-cha* at Manhattan filled in all the blanks to discuss the weather (so windy today) and, the price of groceries (potatoes are so expensive these days), and enquire after all my mothers' siblings and even Rasid-Ahmed's faulty ears.

He was undeterred by Bajee's monosyllabic answers; it was all executed in the name of customer service and rightly so, because to this day, I drive to Fordsburg to patronise Manhattan Dry Cleaners.

Small talk complete, yellow slip firmly tucked into waistcoat threatening to disengage from the tiny pocket it was forced to share with the pocket watch, Bajee turned to my mother. It was the days before thermal vests and, for my mother, being the youngest of five sisters, any warmth originally held in the jersey that she wore had been erased through time and over-usage. My mum grinned at Bajee, shivering slightly.

"*Pooirie waaste?* Something for the little girl?" Bajee turned slightly towards the door, making sure that nobody

Red Riding Hood

he knew was party to this transaction, albeit legal.

The *cha-cha* at Manhattan disappeared behind the curtain and returned with a large pile of unclaimed laundry items. It looked as though these clothes were magically floating towards the counter, but it was his arms holding them all together. He dumped them onto the counter. The rule was that Manhattan would keep clothes for three months and if the owner did not collect an item, it would be sold "to defray costs", usually at a nominal amount.

Both men rummaged through the pile, holding items against my mother's little body, her heart sinking further and further into her shoes as they pulled out item after item clearly intended for an adult. The last thing Bajee pulled out was a red velvet coat with shiny gold buttons. The coat was lined in soft red satin with a collar of faux fur.

"Do you want it? You can wear it now, it will fit you."

"I want to show Ma first."

The *cha-cha* at Manhattan added to the magnificence of the coat by wrapping it in tissue paper and then a clear plastic coat covering with a complimentary wire hanger.

My mother carried that little velvet jacket in her free hand, got home, removed the plastic coating carefully and opened the tissue. The crinkle made her twitch with anticipation. Newspaper was one thing; it served so many practical purposes. Sheets of newspaper served as absorbent material for draining *poori*, damp ones worked a dream with tight shoes and dry ones in spirits made windows blink. But tissue paper was in a league of its own.

As each sister came home, Julie unwrapped and modelled the red velvet coat and then packed it painstakingly back in the tissue paper. It was the day her cravings for the dummy ended. She even felt slightly sorry for Rasid-Ahmed, inflamed ear and all. Vanity conspired with her newfound ownership of the red velvet jacket and she noticed that his vest was a pale shade of pink. Being surrounded by five sisters had its drawbacks. Her mind-set had shifted and she decided that he was to be pitied, not envied.

—

Count your blessings. Such a cliché. My mum says this to me all the time. I tend to listen, agree and pause long enough to draw a breath while detailing the latest misadventure with my sons. She wonders how I would have survived in her childhood home. I am obsessed with privacy, everyone in my home has their own space for self-reflection and growth. I have even dedicated a corner in my house in the pursuit of the very elusive state of self-actualisation.

When my son was three years old, he emptied a three-kilogram tin of Milo powder down the drain because he needed the tin. I placed him on a naughty chair for three minutes, no more, no less, for him to think about what he had done wrong. After three minutes, I stood over him and asked if he had had a good think and if there was anything he would like to say. "Nope, nothing to say, I'm still thinking."

My mother watched this ridiculous strategy play out for 6, 9, 12, 15, 18 minutes. Eventually, utterly defeated, I asked him to get off the chair.

"No," he grinned, "still thinking."

The hunted had become the hunter. My mother watched this unfold with detached amusement.

Red Riding Hood

I believe her when she says that I would not have survived long in Vorster Street, under Ma and Bajee's set of rules. Everyone knew their place and recognised their space in that tiny flat. It was usually where nobody was currently sitting or sleeping. Warm clothes were shared and if it was not being currently worn, it was fair game.

—

My mother sized her sisters up. They were too big to fit into the jacket. She was relieved. The jacket became her biggest blessing. When guests would visit, and after they had been served tea and dipped enough coconut biscuits, she would wait for a lull in the conversation and then stand shyly at the frame of the door waiting for them to notice her.

"Julie? You need something?"

"Want to see something?"

"*Jee pooirie*. Yes, child."

She would run to the cupboard, grab the unreliable stool, balance precariously using one leg and hop on the other to grab the jacket from the top of the cupboard. Her movements were frantic and reckless until she came to the tissue paper. Then slowly, so slowly, she would present the velvet coat for the visitor's approval.

"Yours? *Mashallah*, Julie, *ketloo roopari!*"

Before long, this became her party trick. Right through that winter, she did not notice the bare branches sprouting buds. She did not notice the coats giving way to sleeveless tops with *ijaars* and the *godroos* being packed under the beds. She did not notice that the *Fajr* call to prayer was earlier each morning.

During the December holidays, her distant relatives were passing through Newtown on their way to Durban and stopped, as relatives do, for a cup of tea. A Highveld storm was brewing and, even though my mum and her siblings had never been on a holiday, there was collective excitement and genuine elation at their good fortune. No, they could not stay long, and *takleef maaf* and *Allah hafiz*, and then it happened. My aunt's daughter shivered ever so slightly, but enough to catch Ma's eye.

Without a thought, Ma retrieved my mother's red velvet jacket, using a *vehlin* to dislodge it from its sanctified spot, and it fell to the ground with a thud. The jacket was about to form part of the community of property.

"Here, put this on for her, it's cold."

"Doesn't it fit Julie?"

My mother grabbed it from my Ma's hand in uncharacteristic brazenness and tried to slip it on. How she tried! It simply would not fit.

"What must you tell Julie?"

"*JazakAllah*," and with that, the cousin simply put it on. It was, for her, a coat.

My mother felt all her blessings leave with that Ford Cortina full of jovial distant family. She stared at the car, numb with grief, until it turned the corner.

"Want to play marbles, Julie?" She couldn't help but smile. Ma had bandaged Rasid-Ahmed's head to protect his ears by wrapping the dressing under his chin and across his head.

"Yes, let's play marbles."

Chapter 12

Christmas Beetles

There are two kinds of people in this world. Those who turn Christmas beetles back onto their legs and those who do not. In my observations, people do several things, all quite revealing. My mum likes to flip them over onto their legs: she uses a sheet of newspaper so she does not have to touch them. They are the only insects that get spared the insecticide treatment from her. I think it is the helplessness and vulnerability of the spindly legs.

My husband likes to *relocate* Christmas beetles. This can be annoying mid-supper, mid-teenage tantrum, or mid-Netflix movie. He lifts them up carefully between thumb and index finger, turns them over into the palm of his hand, carries them to the garden and lays them carefully onto the grass. "They can die where they were born." The beetle spends most of its life safely underground and I find it ironic that it lands up in our homes or in our hair as it nears the end of its life cycle.

Then you get people who simply crush Christmas beetles. It must take a special type of person to just step on them. Why do that? We are all optimistic, aren't we? Even if it is going to die, and soon, its chances of survival are infinitely improved if we flip it over, surely? These are the people to whom this sentiment does not even occur.

Christmas time in Fordsburg meant that my cousins and I would converge on Ma's house and have endless sleepovers and pamper-parties. We would wait for an adult to take us for an evening drive up and down Commissioner Street.

The bright lights and changing traffic-lights that started at the Carlton Centre and ended down near Chinatown were a sensory nirvana. At five-storey height, for two kilometres, at every intersection, the colourful lights were arranged in shapes: reindeer, elves, candy sticks and green wreaths. Each intersection had traffic-lights and, suspended above that, three sets of Christmas lights. We all had our favourites and mine was the clown who seemed very out of place in that environment. The drive, in a car full of cousins crammed together with little ones sitting on older cousins' laps, and the feeling that there was no school for weeks on end, made it my most magical childhood experience.

Sometimes, the sky would darken to a forbidding grey, and before any rain fell there would be electric cracks of thunder and we would shriek with excitement. Rain in Fordsburg and near the Johannesburg CBD in the 1980s was different to rain in suburbia nowadays. Now, no matter how hard it rains, the rain sounds polite. In suburbia, rain falls on a tiled roof rather than a zinc roof. In Fordsburg, the rain would come down heavy and hard and we would switch lights on in the house, and then it would pass and the sunshine would glimmer in the puddles.

That sequence of rain followed by humid heat was the signal for us to start racing paper-boats down Vorster Street, which sloped downhill from the mosque. We would race them in the overflowing gutters. The cousin whose boat came in last would be nominated to start nagging an adult to take us for a drive down Commissioner Street. Because we were all female, seniority or leadership would never be decided according to our sex. Two of our male cousins were much older and at university, Riaz had moved with his family to Cape Town, Zunaid lived in Kinross and Shiraz lived in Canada. What was left was an assortment of personalities, all female, and so we devised games like this to sort out the pecking order for the day.

Another popular Christmas ritual in our family was being taken to Wemmer Pan, south Johannesburg, on a night leading up to Christmas. On the grassy slopes of a man-made lake we would picnic and watch musical fountains dance to classical music. Vendors sold neon-green glow-in-the-dark necklaces and helium-filled bunny-shaped balloons. My mum would fill tartan-coloured plastic flasks with fragile glass inners with coffee and task the eldest cousin with keeping them in an upright position for the drive there – because those things broke easily – and make each of us solemnly promise not to ask for the green necklaces or balloons. The drive back to Fordsburg from Wemmer Pan meant going down Commissioner Street and seeing the lights again.

Even though we were quite aware that we were not Christian, we made the most of the free festivities. On Christmas Eve, my mum would carry the plastic pine tree from the display window in her shop in the Oriental Plaza, give it the once-over with a feather duster and place lucky packets as gifts underneath. The pink and yellow packets had a picture of a blonde princess admiring herself in a hand-held mirror and the slogan said, "For a good little princess, what every girl wants ... all girls love dressing up." My mum would turn off the lights in the lounge and plug in a string of flashing lights around the tree. The packets were identical, all seven of them. We would spend hours the next day bartering and negotiating with the contents. Shamila, the youngest, would end up with seven hair clips. Most of us had short hair and she was often negotiated out of the better trinkets.

Of course, Christmas beetles would be attracted by the flashing tree and chose to spend their dying moments with us. We would sweep them out or turn them onto their legs because it is what we saw the adults doing.

On Christmas Eve in 1982, Aunty Farida came to visit. She was different from almost everyone I had met and nobody knew why, but each of my aunties, her cousins, had a different theory. My mum insisted that Farida's great-grandfather on her mother's side was a corrupt farmer in India who would weigh the lentils incorrectly and cheat his customers out of several handfuls at every purchase. When he was found out, the community cursed him with

Christmas Beetles

a malediction that a female child would be born who was so unlikeable and nasty that she would "spoil" the family name. My mum identified her as Farida.

My Aunt Hajira believed that Farida had been an extraordinarily beautiful baby. On a certain night, just as the sun was setting, her mum settled down under a tree to breastfeed her. The giggles from the beautiful baby attracted a sinister spirit. Farida began screaming and crying and has been a miserable person ever since. Despite Farida's claims that she is deeply religious and God-fearing, the demon has never left her.

Aunty Zuby, not one for fanciful speculation, suggested that Farida thought she was the Chosen One because she had been honoured by having a male only child. This belief was evident when she suggested to all seven of us girl cousins that he be given the front seat of the car while the rest of us squeezed into the back. Aunty Zuby would have none of that and Ahmed was never invited again for a trip down Commissioner Street in the car. Whenever they visited, he spent his time on the stoep of Ma's house squashing Christmas beetles.

Aunty Khatija said that there was no explanation for why Farida turned out the way she did. Nothing can save a rotten apple. Every family has one, best we say nothing and hope that her visits are short-lived.

Farida was tolerated by her cousins, who had been socialised into believing that one never corrects or offends a guest. They sucked it up.

On Christmas Eve in 1982, Farida visited Ma's house. Her husband was away on business and she thought it would bring her good fortune to visit her elderly aunt. All seven of us had already left for Wemmer Pan with my mum but the Christmas tree had been set up in the lounge and the lucky packets rested at the plastic base waiting for our return. Her son Ahmed was entranced by the flickering lights, but Farida pulled him away as though the joy would be contagious.

An hour later, we spilled out of my mum's Ford Escort, humming the tune from "Jingle Bells", most of us wearing shorts and T-shirts and pushing and shoving each other as we burst in. As each of us saw Aunty Farida, our tune faltered and we fell silent. My mum, ever gracious, greeted her cousin warmly.

"What a lovely surprise!"

The rest of us formed a semi-circle around them, knowing that the evening had taken a turn for the worse.

"*As-salamu alaykum*, pretty girls! There's so many of you! Julie, which one is yours?"

My older cousin Tashmia shoved me to the front.

"This is your small one? It's a girl, *nê*? You keep her hair so short-short, I wasn't sure. I was just telling Ma that for so long I haven't visited, you all must be missing me so much! Julie, Ahmed only drinks cream soda and I will have a cup of tea. Boiled, *nê*? Otherwise it can't go down."

She patted her chest for emphasis.

My mum disappeared into the kitchen to arrange the special order while Aunty Farida chatted to us. She enquired which of us attended madressa, to which we all put our hands up as children would answering a teacher in class. We stood rooted to the spot, by then also having been socialised into believing that a guest must dismiss one. One cannot ask to be excused.

"Come, let us pray while we waiting for tea."

We lifted our hands and held them together.

"You girls pray without a scarf? What is that! Go get scarves!"

We all scampered to source head-coverings. My sweet cousin Shamila, the youngest, was shoved out of the way and stood staring at the empty scarf drawer. We were a resourceful lot and so she took a checked dishcloth from the kitchen and placed it on her head. Of course, it did not cover her hair; it sat like a piece of dough on a board with the corners covering her ears and the centre point dipping down to her nose. She kept her head tall and her neck stiff to keep the dishcloth in place. We reassembled around Aunty Farida, lifting our hands.

"*Ya* Allah, bless this family. You have sent me here to give them *hidayat* and I have listened to you. I now see why you have sent me.

"*Ya* Allah, bless this family with sons. They have tried and tried but you keep giving them girls. These are good people, *Ya* Allah, have mercy on them. I am asking on their behalf, I am BEGGING on their behalf, your humble servant. These girls standing before me will leave one day, *Ya* Allah. Who will take care of my cousins, *Ya* Allah?"

This last sentence came out very accusatorily. She tried to guilt God.

"I make *dua* to you that they be given a son exactly like you have given Ahmed to me. You have blessed me and now I ask you to bless them. *Aameen!*"

How long does it take to make a cup of tea!

Hearing Aunty Farida say *Aameen* was our signal to end the prayer by sweeping our hands across our faces as one would when washing.

"Did I say I was done? *Ya* Allah, set these girls on the right path. Teach them how to dress so that they cover their shame, help my cousins raise them so that they bring joy to the family they live with ... keep them happy with their husbands, teach them patience and understanding so that You may be pleased with them... teach them that we are not *Nasara* (people of Nazareth), we do not celebrate Christmas, take all the temptations out of this world for them ... keep them away from *haram*, from influences in this world ... let them turn to their parents for guidance ..."

Shamila, who was four, started swaying. She was exhausted and Aunty Farida's sermonising was having a lulling effect. Her head kept dropping and jerking back and she was about to lose the dishcloth. My sister Shahana and my cousin Anisa, 12 and 11 years old, dug elbows into each other throughout the prayer with their eyes closed. Tashmia's face took on the expression of a worshipper in a Full Gospel Church. Of course, it was exaggerated, cocky and facetious. I am sure it must have taken much self-restraint not to throw in a few hallelujahs. While the rest of us stood dead still, she raised her hands to the heavens and swayed from side to side. Luckily, Aunty Farida kept her eyes closed, so taken with her own sermon that she did not notice our responses.

I stood there with my mouth and eyes wide open, staring at this woman who must have a special connection to God

Christmas Beetles

to ask for such specific things. I was six years old and this was the first I had heard about my very existence requiring vehement prayer. Just before she ended, she flicked an energetic Christmas beetle off her neck and broke its shell under her foot. As she ended, we all pronounced the end of the prayer with Arabic inflection, "*Aameen.*" Except for Tashmia who answered a second after all of us with a spirited gospel "*AY-MEN!*" Aunty Farida glared at her a second longer.

All three theories were correct. She was damned, possessed and rotten.

As the years flew by and we grew older, the games we played changed from begging an adult for a drive to learning how to drive. We would now barter with Michael Jackson cassettes and record music videos from *Pop Shop* to be shared on weekends at Ma's house. Eventually, all of us stopped going to Ma's house on weekends when we were at university and the thrill of a campus party and the freedom of being able to drive revolutionised our options.

We would hear snippets about Aunty Farida from our mums and we were told that Ahmed had joined his dad in the family business. On one occasion, Aunty Farida was visiting our home and I parked my little Toyota Conquest in the garage and walked right into the kitchen. For a second I did not recognise her, because she had taken to wearing a niqab, a face covering, which she kept firmly in place because my dad was home. There was no mistaking her syrupy sweet voice, though.

"This your small one, Julie? *Mashallah*! How she has grown! Come here, sit, sit ..."

Her tone was condescending and she examined me from

head to toe as those sweet words were spat out. She took in my faded jeans, sleeveless shirt and Doc Martens with utter disgust. I was only 19 and the themes of my gender studies class were pitted against years of my mum's enculturation, and so for now this battle raged only in my head.

It is a funny thing when one looks back. Until I was about 18, my life had happened mostly in a seven-kilometre physical radius, in Fordsburg. It had been further circumscribed by apartheid. Starting a Bachelor of Arts degree and being exposed to so many new ways of looking at the world had created in me the urge to *transform* the thinking of people who weren't exposed to these ideas. I grappled with this in my twenties. I was angry, I felt cheated and I was going to fight back. But I did not pick my battles well, though as I got older, I learnt to conserve strength for spaces where change could be affected. Basically, people like Aunty Farida cannot be saved and are best avoided.

I sat down next to her with so much enthusiasm, my mum choked on her tea. I thought I would cope.

"Mummy says you at Wits now? So many blacks there, you must be careful. That's why I told Ahmed, rather join your father. You know, Julie, these girls don't listen. Ahmed, one thing, he is good boy. He listens to us. What are you studying? Law? Men don't like it when their wives are too clever, I must warn you. You already 19? Julie! Nice girls coming every year, she will sit on the shelf."

I think in images, so I pictured myself between the condensed milk and Ultra Mel custard in Checkers with a price on my T-shirt.

"I told Rasid-Ahmed the same thing about his daughter

… What's her name … Tashmia … who wants to marry a dentist? You know any sweet girls for my Ahmed? I told him I need someone to help me in the kitchen, arthritis getting very bad.

"Razina, you still don't wear a scarf? If you put one on your head, I promise you will find it very hard to take it off. Your modesty is important and your shame must be covered.

"Julie, do you pray for her? I will send you the right *duas*. You know, without our *duas*, our children are nothing!"

I did not know where to start. Again, the six-year-old in me stared at her open-mouthed, almost not believing that she believed the drivel she was spewing.

I stood up and left the kitchen without greeting. Two acts of defiance right there.

A month later, and towards November, the jacaranda tree outside the library at Wits was in full bloom. Urban legend held that if you had not started studying when the first purple bloom hit the floor, you would fail. I had arranged to meet a friend to swop lecture notes, but Tashmia came running at me.

"We have to go to Aunty Farida's house. Big shit happening."

"You go … I can't. I'm waiting for notes … I missed one lecture in August."

The lone jacaranda bloom at my feet threatened. But Tashmia is very persuasive and within 15 minutes we joined the crowd of 50 family members, friends, emergency vehicles, police and a fire engine along with curious passers-by outside Aunty Farida's home.

There was a long stepladder leaning against the double-storey house and her son Ahmed was standing on the ladder about halfway, looking up and crying and pleading, while her husband paced at the base looking very worried.

Ahmed had told his mum that he had picked the woman he wanted to marry. She was a final-year architecture student at Wits and she was of mixed race. He had been dating her for years and he had broken the news to his parents several hours earlier. His dad was silent but Aunty Farida raged, she spewed fire, she cursed him, she cursed his girlfriend's family, she cursed the day she gave birth to him, she cursed every single roti she had made for him and she cursed her son's unborn children. Ahmed was expecting this. Seeing that she was getting nowhere, she threatened to disown him, and as he was leaving the house, she ran into her bathroom and said she was going to kill herself. This was a bit much for Ahmed, knowing that suicide is considered by many to be a sin in Islam, and he erred on the side of caution and turned around, but it was too late. Farida had slammed the door shut and nobody heard a peep from the bathroom. First, he tried reasoning with her. Then the socialisation kicked in and he started pleading. After his dad called the fire brigade for a long enough ladder, Ahmed started crying and grovelling.

Farida had him exactly where she wanted him. Her manipulation machine was at full throttle. Now what to do with all this attention? She thought to light some candles and run a bath. Wonderful idea! He needs to learn a lesson. Children these days … ungrateful wretches. While she ran the bath, she could think carefully about all the pretty young girls she had met with Ahmed. Nabila was a good bet, green eyes and all, but she seemed a little full of herself, bouncing into the room like that. Yasmin was also nice, but a bit dark in complexion ... nobody wants dark grandchildren; she shuddered at the thought and eliminated Yasmin immediately. Finding a good daughter-in-law for herself was not going to be easy.

Fire Chief Langa sat in the driver's seat of the fire engine. He finished off his cigarette and carefully killed it under his foot as he got out of the emergency vehicle. Watching Ahmed for two hours was getting exhausting, they could be called out at any second to attend to a fire and they would need the ladder. Authoritatively, he walked up to Ahmed's father and they had a few words. He then asked Ahmed to dismount from the ladder, took a deep breath and made his way up. As he came level with the bathroom window, he reached for his hammer and, turning his head away from the shattering glass, swung it into the window. We all heard Aunty Farida scream. He climbed through the window awkwardly while we all held our breath. Of course, it would have made more sense to break down the bathroom door, but she had slam-locked the Trellidor at the top of the stairs inside the house, and breaking that down might have accelerated the suicide threat.

Also, we would all have missed the sight of Aunty Farida slung over Chief Langa's shoulder, naked and wet. He had to step down carefully: she was not a light woman, but thankfully, she did not struggle. The crowd let out a collective gasp of horror and almost all the women who wore scarves pulled them off to cover her as he took careful step down after careful step down. About midway, he looked as though he might fall – he wobbled a bit – and Aunty Farida clung to him more tightly. It took him a full five minutes to reach the bottom.

He got her to her feet and as the crowd broke into applause – it was mainly the passers-by – Tashmia let out an enthusiastic *Hallelujah!*

Ahmed stared at his mother for a whole minute while her cousins and friends threw anything they could find over her. He got into his car and never came back.

Farida is now 70. Her husband passed on five years ago. Her cousins take turns visiting her and they bicker about whose turn it is. She sometimes takes a slow walk down to the shops where she stops to give young people *hidayat*. They look at her as though she is mad. She tries to picture her granddaughters; she was told that they have green eyes. Her days pass in prayer for her son to leave his wife, she waits for all her curses to materialise and when she is really bored, she crushes Christmas beetles.

Chapter 13

Humiliation

The thing about humiliation is that it never truly leaves you.

It is one of those emotions that burn a welt into your brain. Time pushes humiliation deep into the recesses of the brain until you think it has disappeared. But then something triggers the emotion and the blood rushes to your face, the face burns and the heart beats faster. Like the fastest animal in a starving pack, it reaches its prey first and devours logic and reason. I understand humiliation, because it is the emotion that makes one take some of the blame. Anger, by contrast, is a beautiful emotion, it bubbles and has a volcanic quality. When one is justified, the manifestation of anger, correctly channelled, can be cathartic and cleansing. But humiliation sits on your head. It is visceral, crude and public. It is a hot potato that cannot be passed to someone else, or shared. One is singled out and, well, humiliated.

I remember my first day of school well. The week before was spent filling the expensive stationery list, and I have one of those mums who relished covering the books in fancy wrapping-paper and using Letraset to transfer my name onto the books instead of labels. She shopped for glitter and stickers and bought the more expensive markers that contained more than just the primary colours. The first page of every book displayed an elaborate drawing of a flower. Covering books was a family affair, undertaken in one sitting one night after supper. My dad cut the wrapping to size, dozens of sheets, and then did the same with the plastic. On the edge of our dining room table, identical strips of sticky tape lay in a row waiting patiently to be the final steps in the factory of school preparedness. A few times, my older sister leaned against the table, grazing the strips and sticking them all down onto the table – that set us back at least half-an-hour each time. Radio Truro crackled out some Bollywood tune in the kitchen and my mum boiled mint tea and absolutely relished the task that lay ahead. Once the books were covered, there was a final check of the pencil-case, and then finally, my first school suitcase leaned against my bed in quiet expectation of Grade 1. It was a hard, brown suitcase with a handle and briefcase style locks that one could flick open. It made me feel very grown up.

After the obligatory first-day-of-school photo of me leaning against the smartest car in the street, hand on my hip and clip holding the fringe out of my eyes, with a school dress at least two sizes too big, I sat down at my desk, face shiny with excitement. Strangely, I do not recall anybody crying from separation anxiety. We were a brave lot, the class of Grade 1s in 1982 at Bree Street Primary School. It would be years later that the word "humiliation" would crop up in the spelling list and we would have to copy out the meaning from the dictionary and know that Grade 1 had a name all of its own.

Mrs Devar, our Grade 1 teacher, was a hulk of a woman. She arrived unsmiling with her hair pulled back in a tight bun revealing a self-inflicted diminishing hairline and an orange sari. The sari is a beautiful garment. It dances with its wearer: it is like an echo in a love song, the flicker of a fighter fish's trailing tail. That Mrs Devar, with her crude disposition, wore a sari was a travesty – there was nothing fluid or soft about her. By June 1982, I hated the sari almost as much as I hated her. It was *her* uniform. During winter, she teamed it up with a beige knitted cardigan. The black Green Cross sandals were also a permanent fixture. In summer when she wore no socks I spent a fair amount of time following the progression of the fungal infection in the big toe of her right foot.

"Who can write their name?" she barked after roll call on the first day.

I put my hand up and was horrified to see that I was the only one. I had obviously not read the atmosphere accurately. I knew that Sameera Khota could write her name, I saw her do it, why was I the only one volunteering this information? Surely it was a good thing? Mrs Devar signalled for me to take the chalk and pointed at the blackboard. Hesitantly, I wrote my name on the blackboard. I remembered the capital letters and tried to get the small letters in a neat row, painfully aware of 28 sets of eyes staring at me. The chalk squeaked disturbingly as I heard my mum's voice in my head, "The 'a' is round, up and down ... the 'z' is easy, just two lines and then join them ..."

"Razina?"

"Yes, Madam."

"Did your mother buy you the ruler that we asked for?"

"Yes, Madam."

"Bring it here."

I was relieved. I would line up the ruler under my name. I knew the word: underline.

"Hold your hands out. Knuckles up."

The white Penguin ruler bore down on my hands at a 90-degree angle.

Primary school was strange. We had a teacher who hung a naked Barbie doll on the edge of the blackboard and occasionally spoke to her. His eyesight was poor, he wore thick black-rimmed glasses and he positioned his body close to the board, legs apart and bent. By Standard 5, the boys in the class took to biting off bits of paper, chewing them into a masticated mass, loading it into a straw and spitting it onto the board while he was writing. Mr Chagan would identify this as an imperfection on the worn-out board and continue to write, going around the disgusting spitball. Occasionally, a ball would land on his back or in his hair and sit there for the rest of the day. Whichever boy achieved that feat would be elevated to hero status until second break. Mr Chagan was oblivious to questions, comments, good or bad behaviour. It was as though the bell signalling the end of one period and the start of another just meant for him to rinse and repeat. He asked for no respect from his learners and we, in turn, gave him none. I sometimes wondered whether our treatment of him was humiliating, or if he was unaware of it. His humiliation sat in quiet silence in a spit ball on the nape of his neck.

The Group Areas Act denied our parents any options in terms of picking a high school and so my friends and I went to Johannesburg Secondary School, a block away from the primary school, in 1989. The buildings were disintegrating and the fields were sand. A soccer match raised a dusty storm which, mixed with perspiration, made the boys it landed on look as though they had been in an earthquake. There were 1000 pupils crammed into a space designed for 400. The school hall was divided into five classrooms and one could tune in to any subject being taught in that space.

By this time, many families of Indian origin had relocated from Fordsburg and Newtown to the neighbouring areas of Mayfair and Homestead Park. The whites-only high school in Homestead Park was a three-storey face-brick work of art that could comfortably house 2000 pupils, but it served 15 white pupils. It had three grassed soccer fields, a fully equipped laboratory and massive, airy classrooms. There were red velvet stage curtains in the school hall, a sound system with theatre lighting and electronic printing equipment. This changed in 1990, when schools were forced to become racially integrated. As a community immersed in the political atmosphere of the day, we collectively and defiantly left behind the Roneo duplicating machines of

Fordsburg and occupied the space, electronic printers included, in Homestead Park. By the time we settled down, all but four of the school's previous learners had left. The location had changed but we brought with us the name "Johannesburg Secondary School".

My peers and I were juniors in the new environment. We were 13 years old, battling unstable hormones, pimples and puberty, and had survived many years of humiliation at the hands of teachers in primary school. Some had worn the label "troublemaker" with pride. This group arrived at high school with a *dik* attitude. I, on the other hand, had learnt at primary school that if I shut up, did my work and just got on with things, I would have a different experience from the ones who were always being marched off to the head's office. I quietly watched the teachers, reading body language, knowing when to answer and when not to. It was manipulative and insincere, but it had earned me Head Girl status in Standard 5.

Johannesburg Secondary School had a reputation for drugs, fistfights and incompetent teaching. Principals had come and gone within months of each other and on my first day it was easy to see why. Orientation week assembly with the new principal went something like like this:

"OK, so I want to welcome all the new rubbishes from primary school. Don't think that you can come here with a *dik* attitude. We won't tolerate that. If you want to behave like the rubbishes in the higher grades, you will see what we will do with you. This year I am focusing on DISCIPLINE. I'm going to turn things around. I don't take shit from pupils …"

Humiliation

He lost me after the second time he called us "rubbishes". It was going to be more of the same.

Still, I was optimistic. The plan was to just get through this. Feign respect, comply and I thought I would be fine.

The day started with an English class.

"Razina?"

"Yes, Sir?"

"Go hand this list to Mr Bhamjee. He is three classes away."

"Yes, Sir."

Mr Bhamjee's door was closed but he had attached a note saying, "Knock before entering."

I stood outside for a moment and listened to his booming voice barking off accounting concepts. He was louder than was necessary and I waited for him to pause before I knocked but that was not going to happen. He was in full song. I knocked, loudly enough I thought, and waited. No response. The lesson went on. After another two minutes, I knocked again, this time more loudly, and waited. No response. After my third attempt and not wanting to irritate the English teacher with an explanation of how I was not competent enough to deliver a class list, I simply opened the door and walked towards him. He was standing at the blackboard, not even pausing to acknowledge me.

"Good morning, Sir. Sorry to disturb you, but Mr Naidoo asked me to hand this to you."

I held out the class list. Mr Bhamjee continued the lesson as though I was invisible. I glanced over at the pupils to see what was going on and they looked terrified for me. Some looked away in embarrassment and others started smirking.

A HOME ON VORSTER STREET

One pupil right at the back – his choice of seat giving him away – caught my eye and held his right hand in front of him motioning frantically as one would if one had pulled one's hand out of a fire. I could almost hear the rhyme, "You in skits, Marie biscuits!" The ditty makes no sense, it is infantile, but we used to chant this out when someone landed themselves in serious trouble with authority. The chant must go with the hand movement, just like toes must be touched with "This little piggy went to market, this little piggy stayed at home".

With my arm out holding the class list, a huge urge to pee and my face burning, I had no idea what to do. He left me standing there for a full two minutes and then, just as I decided to make a run for it, he addressed me.

"What is your name, you rude child! Did they not teach you how to read in primary school? What does the sign outside my door say?"

Now you cannot blame me for thinking that this was a rhetorical question. I did not answer. It was not. He waited.

"WHAT DOES IT SAY!?"

"Knock before entering, Sir," I barely recognised my adrenalin-fuelled voice.

"OH! So, you CAN read! Very good. Now let's try that again. And this time, you WAIT until I tell you that you can enter."

I stepped out, closed the door, knocked and waited. He let some time pass, as a sadist would, and then, very cheerfully, "PLEASE COME IN". Again, I greeted, apologised and handed him the list. I could not make eye contact with the other pupils in the class and left, closing the door carefully

Humiliation

behind me. I heard him resume the lesson. I ran to the bathroom and cried my little 13-year-old eyes out. In hindsight, me and first days of anything do not go well together.

Humiliation regularly made streams on my clean 8am face and dotted the front of my white school shirt with the fragrance of Oil of Olay. Collectively, all my friends had suffered similar incidents at school. None were exactly the same, it depended on a teacher's reading of the pupil's personality type, family background, grade, physique and whether or not they fitted into the popular kids' crew. Those who were marginalised by their peers suffered doubly because they were easy pickings for the teachers. Like predators, they fed off the weakest link in a particular class. The wittier one was, the less chance of being picked on because then the humiliation could turn on a teacher. Some teachers were close in age to the senior high pupils and they would socialise on weekends, another fail-safe protection against being humiliated. They had each other's backs. Girls who were attractive were subjected to sexual innuendo and flirtation from male teachers, often responding with "*Haai sies*, Sir," and nothing else. We now have words for this type of harassment. In those days, we simply called the predatory behaviour *voor*, or forward.

Enough years of this type of treatment and the tide will turn. The school did have a problem with discipline, but the instigators were those in authority. With no respect for the children, the teachers were playing a game that they had set themselves up to lose.

When I was in Standard 9, Ebrahim Mia walked past Ashan Doshi and looked at him "funny". The biggest point of contention, hours later, with all of us in the principal's office along with the Brixton police, was who looked at whom "funny" first. Both matriculants were towering over the cops, trying very hard to look brave, and the best explanation for the riot they had caused came down to an expression neither could explain.

Mr Naicker, the principal, would regularly enter classrooms and ask everyone to step away from their desks. He, along with two lieutenants, usually the physical education teachers, would search our bags. He called it a shakedown, we called it a raid. Eventually he was so impressed with his confiscated assortment of flick-knives, knuckle-dusters and kitchen utensils that he commissioned a large glass display cabinet in his office to house his markers of competence as a principal. Each item had a date and the grade from which it was confiscated. Parents of difficult pupils would be shown this display cabinet and Mr Naicker would look from cabinet to parent as if to say, *Do you see what I am faced with?*

It was into this glass display cabinet that Ebrahim threw his right elbow before arming himself, Rambo-style, because Ashan looked at him funny. Ebrahim was fuelled by humiliation. He had had enough. Now this is a typical testosterone-style high school punch-up, but with a twist. He went out to the school gates and instantly, everyone who was present picked a side. Can you imagine 300 high schoolers involved in a punch-up? The girls got in on the action by pulling each other's hair, except for Yumna Adam, who was a black belt in karate. Now she really had fun. She was the one who did karate demonstrations from Grade 1 at all the fetes and functions, breaking boards in a calm, controlled environment. By high school her audience was bored. And clearly so was she, because she grabbed with both hands this opportunity to get in there and have a go at whoever was in front of her. As I said, anger can be beautiful. She was the only combatant who knew what she was doing; the rest of us there did some ridiculous pulling and pushing. Many injuries were self-inflicted. Nobody was actually getting hurt.

Mr Naicker made an urgent appeal on the intercom.

"MAYDAY! MAYDAY! I AM ASKING ALL TEACHERS TO REPORT TO THE FRONT SCHOOL GATES URGENTLY. A LIFE-THREATENING SITUATION IS UNFOLDING! MAYDAY! MAYDAY!"

Leaving his office, he activated all the alarms, left his office door wide open and ran up to the school entrance to meet the staff. As he turned the corner, he had to apply brakes sharply. The momentum made his stomach jiggle like jelly while the rest of him was immobilised. Leading the charge towards him were his lieutenants, followed by Mr Bhamjee, another 16 members of staff and, behind them, 300 gatvol pupils.

We were tired of being terrorised and tormented.

Humiliated.

We saw an opening to turn on them and it was magical. Regardless of whether one was in Ebrahim's or Ashan's camp, we were united in our collective hatred of the teachers. We all made way for Yumna Adam as cars would for an emergency vehicle. She was an excellent runner and had the best shot at inflicting serious damage. The staff ran into

Mr Naicker's office, with Mr Bhamjee tripping and being dragged in backwards by his colleagues. They locked the door and frantically phoned the Brixton police while we stood at the windows and doors tormenting them with insults and daring them to address us.

"KNOCK BEFORE ENTERING, MR BHAMJEE!"

The universe has a plan, and fairness and balance sometimes prevail. Mrs Razia Mayet, the eccentric English teacher who loved South African literature and made the introduction that sparked my love affair with Chris van Wyk's work, was absent on the day. She would recite poetry as if she was in the Great Hall at Wits. Ms Fahmida Cachalia, a feminist visionary and Afrikaans authority, simply did not heed the Mayday warning. She was in trouble with Mr Naicker almost as much as we were. He would make unnecessary announcements on the intercom and she would roll her eyes impatiently. We knew whose side she was on. Ms Feroza Patel, the physics teacher who patiently answered my questions about *why* a small boy would climb a ten-storey building and then drop a ball in a vacuum, was on leave. Short of these three extraordinary women, the rest of the tyrants who taught the matrics were locked in the office.

Hours later, as a member of the Students Representative Council, I was privy to the hilarious conversations with the police, the Parent-Teacher Committee and Mr Naicker about how the fight started. Who looked at whom funny remains one of *the* funniest conversations I have ever witnessed.

For months, the humiliation of the incident had the effect of subduing the teachers. Mr Naicker asked to be transferred and left to teach at a school where pupils "understood" discipline. When he conveyed this information at assembly, there were cheers and hugs and whoops of the kind that you would expect at the news that South Africa would be hosting the World Cup. Until the end of Standard 9, every incident of humiliation was held against the bar he had set. I did not think any teacher could surpass that standard until I met Mr Akram.

Mr Akram tried to counter early-onset baldness by growing the hair at the nape of his neck a quarter way down his back. He was a snappy dresser, wearing skinny jeans long before it was the order of the day. Inspired by Michael Jackson's look, he teamed these with white socks, black shiny loafers and a crocheted tie. Systematics, symbiogenesis, species and sclerenchyma all lent themselves to his lisp, but he was kind enough for us to let it go. Calm and polite, he taught biology to us in matric. It took him until August to reveal his violent temper.

Vikram Daya's parents owned a fruit and vegetable kiosk opposite my parents' shop in the Oriental Plaza. We were never friends really, but he and I were born in the same year and we were raised within metres of each other, both sets of parents being shopkeepers. They were a kind and proud family, always declining my mum's invitation to take refuge in our shop when the weather turned. The family would quickly cover their goods with sails as the sky darkened and sit in the tiny kiosk, waiting for the weather to improve. Vikram was soft-spoken and placid, like his parents. His older siblings all joined the business after they had matriculated, so the kiosk was always a hive of activity. Their wares were displayed with love. My dad used this family as an example of raising *good* children. They never used first names without a suffix to reinforce the love between the siblings, wrapping their names in cotton-wool: Vikram-*bhai*, Shilpa-*bhen*.

In the August of my matric year, Vikram did not do his biology homework. He was not the only pupil guilty of this. But he was the only one who did not belong to a crew; plus, his parents were vendors, he was not a particularly good sportsman and he had no interest in Michael Jackson. Mr Akram asked him to leave the classroom, which was up on the third floor. The August wind conspired against Vikram so as he walked out, a gust of wind banged the door loudly behind him. What we witnessed next was an assault with intention to do grievous bodily harm. Mr Akram ran out behind him, grabbed him by his collar, threw him to the floor and then asked him to stand up. With saliva flying everywhere, frothing at the mouth, eyes engorged, he shouted, "I WILL BREAK YOU … YOU HEAR ME? I am going to BREAK YOU!"

He slapped Vikram across his face. It was so hard that it echoed in the large empty biology lab and left a bright red handprint.

"NOW GET OUT! AND DON'T COME BACK!"

Vikram limped out of the classroom.

"Right everyone, turn to page 147."

It happened so fast, it was so uncharacteristic of Mr Akram, we were so naive, the wind was relentless, we were young … and we have no excuse for remaining silent in the face of such humiliation.

Humiliation

It was after Vikram's mum told my mum that his eardrum had ruptured while playing cricket that I called a private class meeting during registration period the following day. The shock had worn off and we were brainstorming the implications of blowing the whistle. An *impimpi* warned Mr Akram of the possible fall-out from the assault before a plan of action was confirmed but, in any case, it was too late. I had told my mum, who told Mrs Daya, who told the new principal, and it was only my name that was involved. Biology was the last double period on a Friday and the lesson went well. We were prepared for the practical assessments which Mr Akram would grade us on the following week. These assessments would contribute to the final matric symbol. Just as the school bell was about to ring, Mr Akram addressed me.

"Razina, stand up."

Everyone stopped packing up.

"So, I hear that you have a big bloody mouth these days. I am not afraid of you; I am not afraid of your parents; I am not afraid of this principal. I will eff you up, understand me. I don't need this job. I will not have a little bitch tell me what I can and can't do.

"DO YOU UNDERSTAND?

"Class dismissed."

I stared at him defiantly, saying nothing. I received a G symbol for my biology practical the following week, the lowest of all the matriculants in Johannesburg Secondary School in 1993.

Of all the humiliations I had suffered at the hands of teachers, this one hurt the least.

Last week, I overheard my mum telling my sons, with much indignation, how her Standard 4 needlework teacher told her that she had "sawdust for brains" and how that scarred her for life. There is no doubt where I get a taste for the dramatic from. My mum subsequently ran several successful dressmaking schools which empowered many women of her generation to earn an income as dressmakers. My older son laughed, saying that the "diss" was lightweight, embarrassing … "Is that the best insult your teacher could think of?"

Humiliation does one of two things. It can make the subject more determined, more resilient and more resolute. Alternatively, humiliation chips away at the psyche until the subject cannot be recognised and the pieces lie in a heap of unfulfilled dreams.

Our 25th high school reunion took place at the school last year. We had not seen Vikram Daya in years, but somebody tracked him down in Australia and he made the trip for the reunion. After he had been expelled from school for gross insubordination, his parents scraped together enough money to send him to family Down Under. He looked up at the third floor and said to me.

"I got a proper *klap* up there … you remember?"

Instinctively, he raised his hand to his ear and his face burnt a bright red. That is the thing about humiliation. It never truly leaves you.

Chapter 14

Covert and Overt

Our family album is filled with captured moments in time, pictures of my dad walking with his friends through the streets of Marabastad, in Central Pretoria. The area was as diverse as Sophiatown and District Six and the Theba family was immortalised in a book about Marabastad for being the first Indian family to install a flushing toilet in their home. Photographers would shout out to my dad when he was walking in the location with his friends and take a photo. A small financial transaction would follow. For a few shillings (a word my dad still uses if something is cheap and he does not want to be remunerated for it – "it only cost a few shillings") those nameless photographers would catch you mid-stride just as they got your attention. I marvel at the talent: having one opportunity at a good photo, while the subject is in motion, without a motor drive and still managing to bring an era to life. Sometimes, as a backdrop you see a *boula* with a woman braaing mielies, or a *muti* shop with the names and lettering of the family business clearly displayed. You know it is a family business because it would end with the words "and sons".

My dad relocated to Fordsburg when he married my mum but he would sometimes long for the jacaranda trees and warmth of his hometown so we would make a trip to Pretoria. By then Indian residents had been relocated to townships like Laudium and Erasmia and there was no social reason to return to Marabastad. Still, we would take an occasional Sunday drive in our beige Ford Escort to a restaurant in the Pretoria CBD called Fisherman's Kitchen. It was a Portuguese-owned business and one of the few outlets that would allow Indian patrons to purchase their food. With the soft velvet upholstery of the car absorbing the smell of vinegar, we would make our way to the Union Buildings to picnic on an old faded sheet and marvel at Sir Herbert Baker's genius. It was many years later that I made the connection between the way the King's Palace sits at the top of Mapungubwe Hill and the choice of Meintjieskop, the highest point in Pretoria, as the site on which the Union Buildings were erected. The Ottomans, the Chinese and the Moghuls had also used this architectural trick for hundreds of years, but the symbolism of picnicking at the lowest level of the landscaped garden was sadly lost on us.

The picnics were no act of defiance. We would find a tree under which to settle, eat our lunch quietly, invariably get stung by a bee trying to make its way into the Sparberry and drive home slowly to Fordsburg. My parents' body language and the way they did not make eye contact with the security guards taught me that we needed to be on our best behaviour and blend in with the background. The idea was to be as unobtrusive as possible. We would watch white families playing with a ball and laughing loudly. We understood, even as children, that we were in Arcadia, the "Playground of Gods", and we were not welcome. I recall asking my dad why we were not allowed closer to the buildings and he said to me that "they" think we will plant a bomb there. It sounded absurd to me. It was like telling me that if I wore yellow, sunflowers would burst out of my head. It was in moments like these that I knew that something in my world was not *right*. I did not have the vocabulary to ask the right questions and, unlike my dad who was raised in Marabastad, I had nothing to compare it to. It was simply the way things were and my parents created a version of normalcy without breaking the law. It is still difficult to articulate how a lifestyle that I accepted then would be wildly unreasonable to me now. Time is a great educator.

Twenty years after we had stopped having picnics at the Union Buildings, I suggested to my husband that we take our sons to the Pretoria Zoo and travel on the Gautrain, both of which would be firsts for them. Yusuf despises zoos, he finds them inhumane and archaic, but I convinced him that it would just be "this one time" and I brought in reinforcements in the form of two nagging toddlers who, until that point, did not know that it was possible to see the animals in their story books live, albeit in a contrived setting.

After an exhausting four hours, one child in a pram and

the other hoisted on my husband's shoulders, we stopped for pink and white soft-serve ice-cream. I wanted them to be immersed in the Pretoria experience and nothing quite does that like trying to outwit the scorching sun by ensuring that not one drop is wasted.

The queue for ice-cream was made up of parents who looked the same as we did. Strands of hair plastered to foreheads when caps were removed, red-eyed from the midday sun and on a short fuse. I took a few deep breaths; this was my idea and nothing was going to ruin it. A little boy in the queue alongside ours started pulling at his dad's shorts. He was barefoot and I wondered how he managed to walk on the concrete pathways in the heat. I smiled at him, but it just made him more desperate to get his father's attention.

He pointed in my direction. "*Kyk, Pa, kyk!*"

I turned to look at the direction he was pointing in, behind me, half expecting to see one of the elephants that my husband so desperately wanted to free. Nothing. The child kept pulling and tugging and I marvelled at how the dad was able to ignore him when he slid his hand into the pocket and the shorts threatened to slide down.

"*Pa! Pappie! Kyk, Pappie!*"

Eventually, his dad looked away from the cell phone.

"*Kyk, die koelie-baba slaap!*"

I never know how to react. And especially how to react to him calling my sleeping baby a "coolie". I was not going to fight with a child. My resolve to create a memorable day was dissolving faster than the ice-cream in my hands. The sun paled in comparison to the heat I was generating. The blood rushed to my face. A cartoon character about to explode.

"Did you hear what the child just said?" So lame. Yusuf touched my arm. He knew that I did not know how to react, but his expression was calm.

Father and son abandoned the queue and made off slowly in the opposite direction, the phone still absorbing the dad's full attention.

My husband and I argued all the way home about what would have been the appropriate way to handle what felt like a hard slap across my face.

More than anything, he was amused by my reaction.

"Have you never been called a coolie before?"

"No, not to my face!"

"But you do know that some people think it."

"Yes, but they aren't allowed to SAY it!"

"It's the same thing, isn't it?"

My husband used to walk down Plein Street in Rustenburg as a child and the cops would stop him and say, "*Hey koelie, wat doen jy in die stad?* – Hey coolie, what are you doing in the city?"

"*Niks, Meneer, ek loop net* – Nothing, Sir, I'm just walking."

It was becoming clear to me that his experiences were very different from mine. He had built an immunity, if that is possible, and had worked all of this out in his head.

Yusuf is an expert at estimating the correct size of clothing to buy for our kids. He holds it up against their backs skilfully, flicks the sleeve against their wrists. *One size bigger*. And he is always right. I drag my kids into fitting rooms armed with the correct size for their age, one size bigger, one size smaller, and promise them sweets if they behave.

It is no wonder that he is the fun parent.

In Rustenburg, Indians could purchase clothing from chain stores but were not allowed into the fitting rooms. One was not allowed to bring an item of clothing back either, once purchased, so it was best to buy bigger and grow into it. This explains why every photo of him in childhood had folded cuffs and wrists. The Indian township, Zinniaville, had a bicycle shop, a material shop and a café. Residents were forced to go into town to buy groceries and clothes and everything else.

Eventually, after the disastrous day at the zoo, he said to me, "What were you going to say to the father? Get his address and send him a copy of Edward Said's *Orientalism*?" He had a point.

As my children got older, it became critically important to me that they be schooled in an environment that reflected my values and beliefs. I wanted better for them, as all parents do, and I am keenly aware of how privileged I am to be able to have these choices.

The first school that my son attended was an international school. In hindsight, this idea was borne of my own insecurity. In my first-year English class at Wits I was asked to read a passage out loud and I pronounced "Champs-Élysées" as "champs" (rhyming with ramps) "Elise" (like the woman's name). It was in the late afternoon, a tutorial with a handful of us, but the master's student who was running the tutorial gently corrected me. Of course, it took three tries before the French rolled off my tongue, but he was obliged to say something because two white girls in the back got the giggles. They were inseparable, dressed alike, preppy and pretty in an uninteresting sort of way. Even the grunge-inspired Kurt Cobain fan who completed his devotion to Nirvana with a permanent sullen expression sniggered. He never contributed to discussions, but he was clearly paying attention because he sniggered. So much for the "woe is me" veneer. I remember the worst part was knowing that I was being laughed at but not knowing why. Nobody of colour in that tutorial thought anything of it. I was 17 and it was so humiliating, my face burnt a bright red. I was a voracious reader but neither Es'kia Mphahlele nor Ahmed Essop had thought it appropriate to add these words to their books and it was the first time I had come across the phrase. In any event, I would have still pronounced it incorrectly.

The law lectures were marginally worse because they were smaller. The first few rows would always be taken up by white students, not because they arrived early but because the rest of us would shrink into the cheaper seats when we arrived. White students would ask so many questions. I learnt quickly that there were two kinds of questions, one for clarity and the other for thinking out loud. So, you could get a *can you please repeat the reference on the law report* question (clarity) or a *what you are saying is that the interim constitution has a limitations section* question (thinking out loud). It was the ease with which they asked the latter that I found unnerving. On the few occasions that I was forced to answer a question directed at me by an over-enthusiastic lecturer, I would start with "I could be wrong, but I think that …" So many of my friends have, over the years, reported similar experiences when they were at Wits. It was 1995 and on an intellectual level we knew that we had every right to be there, but 17 years of conditioning does not fade overnight. We were the poster children of impostor syndrome.

I looked for a school that would give my son the confidence to ask the "thinking out loud" questions and the ability to pronounce French words confidently. I wanted him to recognise himself as a South African Muslim of Indian heritage. If he turned out to be a feminist, all the better. I wanted him to be surrounded by a world that celebrated him. Why I chose an international school is beyond my understanding. In the first parents' meeting, the principal showcased the diversity of the school by using the word "tolerate" five times, and those were parts of the welcome speech that were in English. The rest was in a European language I do not speak or understand. I sat there, looking interested and hoping for the best. What you are trying to do needs to happen organically, Yusuf argued. You cannot save them from the world.

Eventually the efficient school bus service and canoeing as an extramural trumped the concerns we had. I was uncomfortable about the way in which European exploration was taught: it reminded me of my House of Delegates curriculum detailing the heroic acts of Cape Dutch heroes. I was in Standard 5 when I coloured in a black and white image of Wolraad Woltemade rescuing his men from a sinking ship and I felt Racheltjie de Beer's pain when she protected her brother from freezing to death.

One look at the history worksheet calling Arab traders savages and I had my son's transfer cards in my hand by the afternoon. It took several attempts to set up a meeting and we got the impression that the school authorities did not see what the fuss was about. Eventually we got a half-hearted apology and the young history teacher wrote the K-word on the blackboard and told the kids never to use it. It remained on her blackboard for the day. No discussion about why it would be hurtful nor the history of the word.

By the following week, we had enrolled both the kids in a Catholic school whose principal understood how loaded the word "tolerance" was and I made peace with my sons singing hymns in the shower. Brother Mark would bless the children in the name of whomever they identified as God. Muslim children were transported to Mosque on Fridays for obligatory prayers in a school bus emblazoned with the words "In the Name of Mary". The kids would disembark wearing blazers emblazoned with Christ's cross and a variety of hairstyles. The school's hair policy reflected a "relaxed" environment and differences were truly celebrated. I watched as the Head of Religion for the Primary School danced the night away with her little students at the rollerblade disco. Most importantly, the student body accurately reflected the demographic in South Africa. It felt as though we had found home.

Which is why I was alarmed to catch the tail-end of a conversation between Yusuf and my son.

"So then when the practice bomb drill sounded out loud at the cricket tournament, some of the kids said, 'Mikaeel, why don't you just tell us where you hid the bomb and save us the hassle of walking off the field?'"

I get that it was funny. It was also Islamophobic. Maybe in equal measure. He will learn these things in time, Yusuf argued. Organically. And the world will teach him. When I asked my son if he thought it was Islamophobic he said, "Nah, it's just funny". My son and his classmates were 15, so everything was funny.

A year later, a middle-aged white man thought it appropriate to stand over my brown child in a Virgin Active gym to intimidate him into getting off a cycling machine which he wanted to use. There was a queue and he was not going to bother joining it. It is only after my son refused to come with us the next time we went that he told us of the incident. It is not an incident as such: nothing happened. The man had used his position of privilege to intimidate my child. My son got off the machine. No amount of schooling, discussion and awareness had prepared him for experiencing it live.

These experiences will become a part of our children, in their own time, and in their own ways without them needing to hear about our wounds and the luggage of our hurt. In a sense, I needed him to remain on that bike to confirm that I was doing better for him than my parents did for me. It has taken me 30 years not to get off the bike. In time, my son will stand his ground too.

Chapter 15

Victims!

America's Dumbest Criminals was a wildly popular reality series that aired from 1996 to 2000 in 30 countries. It was much more entertaining than *Police File* with David Hall-Green was in the late 1970s and 1980s. At that time what we could watch was so heavily censored by the state broadcaster that a group of television producers co-opted us to help find petty criminals. The designers and enforcers of the crime against humanity in this country were never featured. I remember that the ratings shot up the night of the episode about André Stander, a South African police captain turned bank robber, who successfully completed 30 bank robberies. It rivalled the viewership of the "Who shot JR?" episode on *Dallas*. Explaining the appeal of this show to anyone born after 1990 is embarrassing.

America's Dumbest Criminals, on the other hand, had all the elements of appeal. It is a cops-and-robbers show, often with live footage and always has a comical angle. My favourite episode was about a bank robber who tried to jump over the tellers' counters, but he underestimated the height, hit his head and knocked himself out cold. So much bravado, so many threats and then he knocked himself out. In another episode, a man who was out on bail for the theft of a motor vehicle stole *another* motor vehicle to get himself to court for trial. His explanation was that he was in enough trouble without defeating the ends of justice by skipping bail.

I do not know any criminals personally, but even so, this kind of behaviour seems irrational and illogical. Like most South Africans, though, I do know people who have been the victims of criminal behaviour. I receive an email every month from my armed security provider detailing how I should behave in the event of a hijacking or robbery and I am told that this advice is the culmination of research, with input from security experts, criminologists and the police. There is apparently a blueprint of behaviour that increases one's chances of survival. Watching *Carte Blanche*, paging through magazines in dentists' reception rooms and reading newspapers online, I have read many ten-point summaries; and the central objective is not to antagonise the criminal. Do not argue, make sure that your hands are visible at all times and speak in a calm, clear tone.

The authors of articles like these have not met my family. Forget the fight or flight response, the fight, flight or *argue* response is what we do.

Victims!

Late on a Friday afternoon, my husband I were driving down Commissioner Street in the Johannesburg CBD. We had bought an inexpensive, old, but flashy, gold Pajero, naively thinking that we would explore every corner of South Africa in it. At the time, we did not know that servicing it would cost nearly the same amount as the purchase price, nor did we know that replacing a Tiptronic gearbox was comparable in price to purchasing a new sedan. I had reservations about driving a 4x4 as I thought it would increase our chances of being hijacked, but Yusuf reassured me that any criminal worth his salt would know that the resale value on this vehicle was a pittance. Also, I did not like the colour.

Most of the traffic lights were out of order, so traffic was at a standstill. The sun was setting behind the bridge between Chinatown and Johannesburg Central Police Station and we were heading westward, so we squinted our eyes against the glare. I found myself getting very animated, pointing out landmarks of my childhood: "See, we would burst crackers for New Year's there," and "All the businessmen would meet for drinks there" and my husband, bless him, was getting more and more agitated with the heat, the traffic and my non-stop romanticising of a city whose past laws ensured that it was a brutal place to raise children. He had heard these stories before, but I was in my element all over again. Sometimes, spouses should listen simply because the storyteller is having such fun.

Suddenly, a man jumped onto the running board of our 4x4 Pajero, stuck his head through the partially opened window and said to my husband, "Give me your phone!"

He was sweating and held something black in one hand. There were cars in front of us and behind us but he stuck to the Pajero like Spiderman. I was expecting my husband to reach into his pocket and hand his phone over, but he glanced at the thug and said in a *VERY* pleasant tone, "Sorry boss, no odds today," and turned his attention back to the road.

The thug and I exchanged confused looks. Did my husband misunderstand? This was a robbery and the guy was armed. All ten points came back to me.

Point #1: Stay calm.

"Umm ... Yusuf, he is asking for your phone." I was certain that there was a misunderstanding. My husband had no idea that we were being held up and that the gun was centimetres away from his head. In fairness, the gun was not visible to Yusuf. The thug was short and had a low centre of gravity. If we had been in a sedan, he could have pointed the gun directly at us. But he needed to stand on the running board AND hold on to the 4x4 AND point a gun at us. Something had to give. He simply did not look threatening enough.

Also, the window was only half open and only half his head was in the car. For a split second I thought of closing the window electronically. That might force him to take his head out to avoid being decapitated. But then I remembered Point #2: Do not antagonise the criminal.

"Sorry Boss, I don't have a phone." By now Yusuf was aware that we were being robbed but his apologetic demeanour and calmness were unnerving me. He actually shrugged and lifted both his hands up to indicate that he dearly wished he had a phone to part with, but sadly, this was not the case.

I looked over to Yusuf and I said, "Do you really expect him to believe that you drive this fancy-ass GOLD Pajero but you don't own a cell phone!"

By now this had nothing to do with the thug. It was a spat between husband and wife and he was caught in the crossfire. He looked at Yusuf like, *Yes! How stupid do you think I am?* But he had one line and one line only. "Give me your phone!"

Yusuf was clearly not going to budge; he kept his eyes straight ahead and we had reached an impasse of sorts. Even if traffic started moving, it would not help, because the guy's feet were not on the ground. For a second, I imagined driving all the way home with him hanging onto the side of the Pajero because we had reached a deadlock. There was no room to negotiate.

"OK, look..." I said to the guy. "...You can take my phone. It's not as fancy as his, but it works really well, in fact it takes better pictures."

I stiffened my legs and lifted my bum off the seat to reach into my jeans pocket and hand the phone over. Of course, I was shaking uncontrollably and as I tried to pass the phone over the Tiptronic gearbox, it fell out my hand and landed between Yusuf and me. Immediately we both bent over, each slightly angled to the gearbox, to retrieve it and we banged our heads together hard. Yusuf retrieved the phone and handed it over and the thug had to do this hop-off move, which was pretty slick because between the gun and him holding on to the Pajero, he was short of a hand to receive the phone. He disappeared into the Friday afternoon rush of jaywalkers and hooting and taxis, but I am certain that we made him consider, at least for a short time, a different career path.

My mum and my husband are very different people. If Yusuf's mantra is "Don't stress," my mum's mantra is "Stress all the time in case something comes up that justifies the stress." She is hyper-vigilant when it comes to safety and regularly cuts out articles from *The Star* with the same ten-point summary. When we visit her, she offers it up as interesting reading material while we wait for the kettle to boil.

Booni Seleke has been my mum's helper for 15 years. Over the years, she has nursed my mum through empty-nest syndrome, tasted countless batches of *adoo masala* to test for heat and served as the final word on whether or not an outfit made my mum look fat. They would often bake together and, as the biscuits came out of the oven, sample the ones that were less than perfect. Towards the end of every year, my mum would go shopping with Aunty Booni for Christmas clothing for her kids and they would come home exhausted but eager to show my dad what they had bought. He could not have been less interested but again, this is one of those times that he knew to pay attention because my mum could make a day of shopping sound like climbing Kilimanjaro.

Aunty Booni and my mum bickered constantly. I am tempted to say that they bickered like an old married couple but that would be denying the inherent power imbalance in relationships between employers and domestic workers in South Africa. There was a ten-year age gap between them.

Victims!

The arrangement was that she would call my mum by her first name, Julie, but if she was annoyed with her, she would call her "Ouma", knowing that she was dealing her a blow. My dad, who she called Ally, often mediated disputes when a lost item was miraculously found, often by him, and the blame game would begin. Both Aunty Booni and my mum would deny having put the scissors in the laundry cupboard when they both knew that it stayed in the top-left kitchen counter. My dad was an expert fence-sitter and struggled to answer the rhetorical question they would both put to him, "Now why would I put it in the laundry cupboard when I KNOW it stays in the kitchen drawer?" Aunty Booni was sometimes his ally but could turn on him quickly depending on which person's point of view suited her at that moment.

"Sê vir Ally dat dhal en rys nie goed vir sy gesondheid is nie. Hy gaan netnou sterf!"[2]

We all know the pile of dishes that making this wholesome meal generates.

It was on an ordinary day that I chose to visit and for no special reason. The kettle was on, Aunty Booni was having tea in her room and my dad had gone out for the day. My mum passed me a newspaper cutting and went to answer the door. She returned to the kitchen with an empty two-litre milk bottle and told me that a man had run out of water for his car and needed help. Thankfully, he passed the bottle through the wrought iron decorative gate and she could pass

---

2 Tell Ally that dhal and rice is not good for his health. It is going to kill him before long!

it back through the gate. I distinctly remember her telling me, "These are the kinds of scams you have to watch out for: he is hoping that I open the gate and then he will attack me."

So why the hell are you entertaining this request?

Apparently, God disguises angels as criminals and tests his servants in this way. And a sure way of finding oneself in hell is to refuse a request of water. There are no guidelines as to how one differentiates between angels and criminals.

Half an hour later, just as I was about to leave, a young woman rang the doorbell. She was holding a giggling baby and asked if she could please come in to change the baby's nappy as she could not do it in the street. As my mum unlocked the gate, her accomplice – the same man who had run out of water and who had been hiding behind the wall – pushed my mum inside, threw her to the ground violently, pointed a gun to her head and told her not to scream. As I walked towards the small area between the gate and the front door, he hit me over the head with the butt of a gun. Now I am familiar with the expression "seeing stars" but unless one has had this experience, it seems just a metaphor. But I *saw stars*. Your eyes are open but there is blackness and little flecks of light dancing in a random constellation like an evening sky in Magaliesberg. Then the blackness clears and reality comes into focus. The only other time I had had this sensation was when my baby boy had downed his night-time bottle and flung it into my face. It was also the night he learnt how to swear.

This man, shifty-eyed and muscular with intimidating height, had everything going for him. We knew that we stood no chance against him. He dragged me, banging my head against the walls, as he made his way around the house with my mum begging him not to hurt me. I chose to say nothing in case it agitated him further.

"Money! Quickly, give me money and jewellery."

"OK, that's in my bedroom." My mum had calmed down enough to understand what it was he wanted and she gestured towards the room at the end of the passage.

She walked quickly to her bedroom door, which was closed. As she slid the handle down and took a step forward, her body banged into the door. She knocked loudly and looked at the man. Shifting her eyes between the door and the man, she kept banging, more desperately.

"Booni? BOONI! Are you in there? Please open. This man wants my handbag."

"No."

"BOONI ... please."

"No."

"Booni, he is going to kill us."

"No."

My mum looked at the guy and shrugged and lifted her hands and I had déjà vu picturing Yusuf doing the exact same thing in town months earlier. They were standing close together, the man and my mum, and she had to tilt her head back to make eye-contact with him he was so tall. At some point, she rolled her eyes at him, her body language saying, *Look here, I'm banging, pleading. What more can I do?* I thought to myself that this was not going to end well. My head was throbbing but there was another feeling of absolute dread. My mum and Aunty Booni were about to argue.

Mum stood with her hands on her hips and looked at the

man, who also did not know what to do. So he hit me over my head again. Thanks a lot, Mum.

"How about we go to my old room next door and all of us jump out of the window and then Aunty Booni can throw things out and he can leave?" It seemed very unfair that the person with the head injury was doing the critical thinking.

All three of us did exactly that and then my mum started explaining to Aunty Booni which handbag in her room held all the treasures.

"Now it's that brown bag that looks like leather but isn't leather. It's the one with the gold studs. Don't give the black one ... The brown one."

Aunty Booni did not respond but a black bag came flying at all of us. My mum ducked slightly.

"This is the problem, she never listens! Not this bag, I said the BROWN bag!" Again, the shrug and eye-roll at the man. What did my mum want from him? It looked a lot like sympathy.

I am certain that this man had witnessed hysterical crying, prayers to Jesus and pleas for life. I do not think that he actually wanted to take my life, but my mum was leaving him with very few options.

"BROWN, BOONI, BROWN!"

The brown bag came flying out and the man released me with a final warning that if we screamed, he would shoot. He started running towards the gate, still pointing the gun at us and my mum.

"Wait ... that bag has my house keys and ID book. Do you know what a pain it is to replace that? That queue at Home Affairs?"

She had touched a nerve.

"Please give it here so that I can take that out."

As God is my witness, the man stopped and walked back to her. He held the bag open while she rummaged through and retrieved those items. I am sure that I heard her thanking him, but she fervently denies having done that.

Of course, we all received trauma counselling, drank tea with visitors and offered prayers of thanks to God for sparing our lives. My mum's recollection of events paints her as so much more of a victim than she has the capacity to be, but Aunty Booni cried the loudest and lay on her bed in her room for days.

By then it had been confirmed for me that my family were terrible targets for crime operatives.

The fight/flight/argue response to crime that my family subscribes to visited my home again many years later. My son had moved to a different school and iPads were required as a learning tool from Grade 7 onwards.

"Could we apply for an exemption excusing him from using this device?"

"Now Mrs Theba, if affordability is an issue …"

"It's not that. I know that he is definitely going to lose it."

"Maybe you need to TRUST in him. Kids these days are so much more responsible than we were … and tell him that it is very expensive."

I used the same school tie from Grade 1 to matric but I replaced a school jersey for my son four times in one year. I have a theory that technology makes kids stupid, and now a device was going to accompany my son all day. I grinned through gritted teeth and put the receipt up on my fridge with instructions for it only to be removed when he matriculated. I threatened to make him use his allowance until he had paid us back if he misplaced it. He would be a grandfather by then and I would be dead. Every morning I would remind him to look after the iPad. *Keep it on you all the time. Use your locker.* It was insured but we did not tell him that.

It took all of three weeks in the new school before I received a call from him while waiting for him to come to the car.

"Mum, somebody stole my iPad."

"WHAAT? WHERE ARE YOU? I'm coming."

I had to ask twice where he was because I did not think the school would have an entire room dedicated to information technology. As I entered, the principal and head of IT stood up to shake my hand.

My son looked positively terrified and I would have told him not to worry, that the device was insured, but he started speaking quickly.

"Mum, the school has closed circuit TV cameras EVERYWHERE and we caught the guy on screen. It's a little blurry, but I think we can find him. He picks up my bag, Mum. It's the one with the orange tick, the Nike one."

The principal piped up.

"Mrs Theba, I know that you are new to the school, but I can assure you that this has never happened before. We take this kind of thing very seriously. Have a seat, I will dim the lights and show you the footage. The boy's face is obscured, but by the end of the school day tomorrow, we will find out who has the iPad."

The principal cleared her throat and talked me through the video.

"So, at exactly 12:22pm, you will see a young man walk toward the bags and pick up your son's bag and walk away. We don't have his face on camera, but we will figure it out."

We started watching and sure enough, I could see exactly what she described. There was just this one little thing. Small but significant. Could they please run the footage again?

They obliged and I kept looking at my son's face for anything ... something, please. Nothing.

"Can I please have a minute with my son?"

"Sure, Mrs Theba, I'm sure that he is very traumatised. So young and the victim of crime ..."

They left the room. I played the clip again.

"DO. YOU. NOT. RECOGNISE. YOURSELF?"

"No, Mum, it's not me."

"DO. YOU. NOT. RECOGNISE. YOURSELF?"

"But Mum, I would know if it was me."

"IT'S YOU."

"No, Mum, that is not me."

"IT'S YOU. I GAVE BIRTH TO YOU. I KNOW."

"But Mum."

It was the shuffle, it was the teenage awkwardness, it was the non-criminal saunter. I could tell by his body language that he had no awareness of what he was doing. It was my son.

He forgot that he had moved his bag to another classroom at some point. He genuinely thought that it had been stolen.

I mitigated his embarrassment by suggesting that I take a walk around the school with him on the off-chance that the culprit dumped it somewhere before a full-scale investigation was launched the following day. We found it under the desk in his maths class, stuck to the story of the culprit growing a conscience and drove home in silence.

I suppose I should be grateful that at least someone in our family knows how to play the victim properly.

Chapter 16

The Wedding

I got one thing right about my wedding day: once the date was set, I claimed very little ownership over the process. Unlike many of my friends, I conceded early on that my parents were paying for the reception, it was their function and this was an opportunity for them to host their relatives and friends. I was happy to be invited.

I did, however, raise my eyebrows at their choice of wedding videographer: a man who had made a career change from being a criminal attorney to a wedding planner after being hit on the head with a brick by his client.

"This guy looks shady," I said to my dad.

"Don't be silly, it could happen to anyone."

"Fine. Just tell him not to put my face in a flower when he prints the pictures."

I recalled the hysterical wedding videos of the 1980s – hundreds of them – to which some of my cousins had fallen victim. They would start with dramatic Hindi music and the couple would be splashed across the screen in twirling configurations. This would be followed by their names and the wedding date, in a gory font on a backdrop of the Okavango Delta or a Hawaiian beach. The bride would be asked to smell a rose – it's always a rose – and the groom would stand aside while the bride interrogated the bud in a bid for the perfect photo. The scene with the groom greeting his mother after *nikah*, the official Muslim wedding ceremony, is done paparazzi-style, with a long-lens camera, to tell a story of the anticipated relationship between mother-in-law and daughter-in-law. I have seen mothers-in-law clinging to their sons, sobbing, while the bride feigns disinterest, too shocked to make a dash for the nearest exit. The groom then generally approaches the bride and plants a virtuous kiss on her cheek, mindful that the music for the delicate lifelong dance between wife and mother has started playing.

Like a well-coordinated orchestra, the food is brought out in courses. Male cousins double as waiters for the day, screaming "More meat, more potatoes, more *paapar*," across a 1000-seater hall into the kitchen, as if the louder they scream, the more important the guests will feel.

Somewhere in the middle of the recording the videographer pauses the tape, usually when the bride's mouth has contorted into looking as if she has suffered a stroke. It is that one mouthful of biryani that she has brought herself to eat that gets captured for time immemorial.

The moment after the revelry, when the bride says fare-

The Wedding

well to her parents, is usually accompanied by a gut-wrenching melody by Lata Mangeshkar about leaving home, with the groom promising to bring his bride back to visit her parents. These songs were written at a time when villages were hundreds of kilometres apart but three generations later in an adopted country the formula is exactly the same.

I had resigned myself to most of it. My only request was that I be spared the rose shot. I would attempt the photo with any flower, but not a rose. I pictured the attorney, who doubled as the wedding planner, packing the equipment for my wedding. Extension cords, lights, camera, lens and rose.

"What is your obsession with flowers?" My dad was irate. "Just let the man do his job." I could've explained how it was too much of a good thing, but roses it would be. I would only be living with my parents for fewer than 100 days and I had begun counting my blessings, acknowledging that I would actually miss them when I left.

My mother started rejoicing at the cupboard space my departure would create and she reminded me that the time had come to take my pots. The pots were purchased by my father when he was a travelling salesman and I was two years old. Having procured the stock at a steal, it made sense for him to keep sets for his wife and for his toddler daughters for when they got married. The seller engraved my name in the pots in Gujarati before I could write it in English. While I was growing up they served as a physical reminder of the sheer quantity of food I would one day be expected to cook. When he brought them home for the first time, I could fit into the largest one comfortably.

Expectations were high. If the pots were there to cement

our roles as home-makers, they were tempered with piles of books to encourage a tertiary education.

"You must read, Razina. It will make you clever." My father again. Before Amazon and Exclusive Books there was the Johannesburg Public Library. Here I was introduced to Zozo and the Man with the Yellow Hat, Enid Blyton and the Mr Men books. My first growth milestone, and one that mattered, was being allowed to take three books home instead of two. Every Saturday afternoon for years, we would walk to the library from our house in Fordsburg and he would hold me over the fountain with the sculptures of three men and allow me to dip my hands in the water. Neither of us could swim and at the age of seven I could count the number of times I had been in a swimming pool on one hand. The water felt ice cold on hot summer days and the ritual felt rebellious in a park where we weren't allowed to sit. The benches near the Impala Stampede in Joubert Street were also off limits to us.

"Which books should I take?"

I would place a few children's books in a neat row on the floor and ask my dad to help me choose.

"*You* decide."

"Yes, but which one looks nice?"

"They all look nice. Pick the ones you think look the nicest and then next week you can take the others."

This is the thing about my father. He would never make choices for me, teaching me from an early age to trust myself. This is possibly why I allowed the videographer – it was unusual for him to want something so badly.

As I grew older, it struck me that my dad was unusually

The Wedding

permissive compared to my friends' dads. I was robbed of the titillation of rebellion.

"What is the name of the place? Let me just write it down." My dad floundered for his glasses.

"C-A-E-S-A-R-S P-A-L-A-C-E"

"Got it! What time will you be back? What's the number at this place? Can I phone to ask to speak to you?"

"No, it's a NIGHTCLUB, Dad." I was hoping to provoke a reaction. I was 17 and in my first year at Wits.

"OK, be home by 10pm latest and be safe."

I would sit there glum and saddled with the knowledge that they knew exactly where I was, drink a Coke and be home before 10pm. I was that kind of a teenager and he was that kind of a father.

Preparation for my wedding went off seamlessly, largely because of my ambivalent attitude. A gown was purchased off-the-peg in one painless afternoon and hung in my cupboard the night before the wedding.

"Try it on for us!" My extended family had arrived and wanted a preview. It was a beaded bodice with a net skirt, classic and simple.

Aunties and cousins poured into my room and stood there in stunned silence. One auntie unconsciously raised her hand to her mouth and took in a sharp breath. Quickly they all left in search of my mum. I heard a commotion of whispers in the passage and then my mum burst into the room, looking distraught.

"It's not actually SLEEVELESS, it's a CAPPED sleeve," she mumbled, "Isn't it?"

Never has three centimetres of fabric, or lack thereof,

plunged so many women into such utter chaos.

"Does it literally not look nice or are they using it as an expression, as in 'It won't look nice to send her off in that gown'?" I was starting to worry. I couldn't tell which answer was worse.

"It won't look nice" is a popular expression amongst our community. It refers to patterns of behaviour, like visiting without bringing baked goods or sending an invitation via email or WhatsApp. It had nothing to do with the physical appearance.

A plan would be made. An old greying burka would be taken apart and stitched to look like a shawl to cover my shoulders. The effect of this cut and paste would cover three centimetres of flesh, save my reputation and ensure that I was liked by my mother-in-law. After an hour of executing this genius plan, I tried on the wedding gown. At that moment a group of children ran through my bedroom. It was past their bedtime, but they were euphoric on unsupervised quantities of Coke and had caught a second wind.

"Auntie Razina, you look like Wonder Woman!"

No, something else was needed.

More consultation. The burka was dismantled and sewn into long thin gloves that rose up to my armpits, leaving the overall impression that I had escaped from a mental institution and managed to partially destroy the straitjacket.

Months of my trying to please everybody dissolved in an ugly cry. I crumpled to the floor and sobbed. My aunts had me believing that revealing three centimetres of my upper arm was akin to tattooing a swastika on my forehead. It was both unforgivable and permanent.

The Wedding

My dad burst into my room, not knowing the source of my hysteria.

"What happened? Why are you crying?" The funny thing about my father is that, in a moment like this, he will not hug me or console me or express any understanding of my feelings. Instead, he tries to understand who has caused this reaction and then holds a vendetta for life. Also, he hates to see me cry.

"Everybody hates my dress!"

"Do *you* like your dress?"

That moment had nothing to do with the dress. His question was an eleventh-hour attempt at teaching me how to trust myself, as he had for so many years.

I wore the wedding gown without any alterations. I had remembered who had raised me.

Chapter 17

Yusuf & Mikaeel

I thrive in a well-structured predictable environment. So much so, that a psychometric assessment revealed that my personality was well-suited to a career in the military. I chose to study logical, reasonable and rule-bound law. Why would I marry a man whose idea of nirvana is to buy a subsistence farm and fish off the banks of his stream? This is Yusuf's idea of heaven. Sadly, he became a city advocate, which put to bed any notions of waking up to farm-fresh living. We met at university. I attended all my lectures, while he sat under a jacaranda tree lecturing on the finer points of tying flies to his fishing friends.

He was not keen on us having children. There are already enough people on this earth. That was his logic. And besides, children come with their own personalities. "They are not as pliable as I am," he would tell me, "and you may not get your way all the time." That should have been enough to put me off. I was undeterred. I was going to raise outstanding little mini-mes. There is a book for everything, I told him. And there's Google.

My better half had foresight. Any unpredictable behaviour sent me sprinting to a book called *What to Expect: Toddlers* by the authors of *What to Expect When You're Expecting*. My mother-in-law, who looks at my style of parenting with some ambivalence, wryly remarked, "I don't know why you keep reading these books. They prey on the fact that you clearly have no idea what you are doing." Ouch!

The differences between us were amplified when we had children. Yusuf's style of parenting fluctuates between telling me to "relax" and telling the kids, "Listen to your mother," thereby pre-empting war. When my son, Mikaeel, broke his arm at school, he looked me in the eye and said softly, "Phone Dad." My son knows me well: the more anxious I get, the less helpful I become. "Is it sore? How sore? Does it feel broken? How broken? Do you need the loo? Rather just go to the loo before we go the hospital. On a scale of 1 to 10, how bad is it?" He looked at me again, this time, desperate. "Please ... Just ... Call ... Dad."

Just as well I called. As we were getting Mikaeel into the car, broken elbow and everything, I slammed the car door into his broken arm. Father and son had a *mashwara* to consult about whether I should even go with them to the hospital. Muttering under their breaths, they begrudgingly agreed that I could, on condition I did not say or touch anything.

Before I became a mother, I would look at children who had cavities disdainfully. How negligent can a mother be? "Make it a non-negotiable," I would think to myself. Nothing would prepare me for how I would grovel and implore my own children to brush their teeth. I naively thought that I had won that battle until the dentist told me that my son had nine cavities. It felt as though I was inflicted with a psychiatric disorder that week. I muttered to myself all day. "Nine, nine, nine." To this day, the number nine holds special significance for my damnation. My husband's expectations were much lower. He was proud that his son allowed a dentist to look into his mouth without the dentist being injured. People who rely on their digits avoid my children; the last hairdresser had to have five stitches sewn between her index finger and thumb.

Part of my madness as a mother was my emphasis on reading. I was the Patron Saint and my son the Worthy Cause. And read I did. I started when he was two months old, and not just kids' books. Instructions for car seat adjustments, recipes for malva pudding and even dry-cleaning tags were not safe from my sermons. Mikaeel is now in his teens and he despises the printed word. *My Best Friend's Smelly Fart* is about the extent of his reading repertoire. And the book is illustrated, hardly what I had hoped for. Despite my fears that I was raising a delinquent, my husband said I should be grateful that his favourite reading was not *Playboy*. Relax.

Germs were another source of angst for me. I would sterilise their bottles until they were two years old, then microwave for a second baptism. My kids knew never to touch buttons on a lift or hold arm rails. "Those never get wiped," I would warn them. On an outing to a pizza place I noticed that my then four-year-old was unusually quiet. As I chatted to friends, he emerged from under the table chewing something. It took me a minute to realise that our food had not arrived. After prying his mouth open, I found an assortment of gum that other patrons had stuck to the bottom of the table. With surgeon-like precision and a well-developed pincer grip, he had managed to dislodge all of it, Stimorol, Clorets, Airwaves. The overriding smell was Chicks Purple. I pinned him down to the floor, World Wrestling Federation-style, straddled his little body and shoved my fist down his throat to extract the last of the gum.

I cannot be anything but dramatic on an ordinary day, but on this day, I was exceptional, my rant was magnificent. I dragged my little bugger into our house and raved about the incident to his dad. His response was incredulous, "They still make Chicks Purple? Mikaeel, how were those PURPLE ones?" I juggled thoughts of unmentionable, unpronounceable diseases and yet nobody was the worse for wear. It was also the year my son did not have a single cough or cold.

My husband is, without a doubt, the better parent.

He is the more popular parent, the more frustrating partner to someone like me. He instinctively knows my sons' needs. I have never said to my kids, "Wait until your father gets home." In fact, they look forward to him vindicating them. I often worry about them being raised in a home with no sisters. "Will they value women? Are we raising sons with a social conscience?"

Yes, I do worry too much. Is it worth it?

I asked my younger son, Amaan, my ray of sunshine, to write a Mother's Day card for my mum. With the sure-footedness of a mountain goat, he wrote, "Dearestest Naani, you (are) the buzz of the bees in my heart. And you cook biryani for me and I know it is full of love."

It is undeniably worth it. There are no rules except the ones we choose and I am learning to live with the fact.

Chapter 18

Amaan

"You will write about this someday," the psychologist said, as he passed me a tissue. The tears trickled down and I blinked at the unfamiliarity of the feeling. It felt like the seconds before collision in a car accident. Of course, there is sheer terror, but there is also a type of calmness, knowing that short of protecting your head, the next few seconds are truly out of your control. The tears dropped out of my eyes into my lap. When the last drop fell, my cheeks were dry and my lap was wet. I was still and so was he. We did not look at each other. In my peripheral vision, I saw him wiping a half tear as he cleared his notes and I wanted to hug him, but I was sure that there are rules about these things. I took in a deep breath. I even felt a little bad. How many sad stories must he have heard? And I made him cry.

A HOME ON VORSTER STREET

—

The gynaecologist swept the ultrasound rod across my stomach for the third time and tried to keep the banter up, but his words were coming out in a stop-start way and his eyes did not leave the screen. He kept pushing buttons and readjusting and realigning and zooming in and out; I stopped talking in case I broke his concentration. There was a frustration in the way he was banging the keys, as though if he banged hard enough the machine could change the result. At one point I felt like telling him, *You tried that, it is showing you the same thing.* Eventually, he abandoned his recommendations for the best street vendors he had eaten at in India and both our eyes fixed on the small monitor. My gynaecologist and I had bonded during my previous pregnancy over our love of Indian food. He was an elderly man and every time he slipped into Gujarati and I responded with the broken bits that I remembered, he would smile broadly. At the end of my previous pregnancy, I asked him if I could ask a question and he responded with "It is your body. If you want an elective Caesar, then an elective Caesar is what you will have." I fell in love with him.

This time, I could see what the problem was. As sophisticated as the equipment was, and as much as I would on previous occasions lie about how I could see the mouth and the penis, the print at the bottom of the monitor needed only basic literacy to decode. My son's head was growing at a rate appropriate to his gestational age, but the rest of his body had stopped growing. Asymmetrical intrauterine growth retardation. Basically, he explained that this meant that my son was not getting the nutrients he required to thrive because of a problem with the placenta or umbilical cord. For now, and quite miraculously, the foetus would direct the energy he was getting from me to maintain growth in his brain and heart at the expense of his liver, muscles and fatty tissue.

He held my hand and took the time to explain what this was, how he planned on monitoring the pregnancy, how I should not stress, and he asked if he should call my husband. He did everything an outstanding healthcare practitioner should do, but he could not change the facts. I was not sobbing. I just could not stop the tears from flowing even though my facial expression held steady. This being our second child, the novelty of gynaecological visits had worn off and I had insisted, when my husband offered to accompany me, that this would be a routine visit. It was when I stepped into the now jam-packed waiting room of uncomfortable-looking pregnant women that I realised that my consultation had been an hour long. Today, the sign that read "Please be patient, next time it could be you who needs the extra love and care" *was* about me. The looks on their faces told me what my face must have looked like. Some smiled as I waited to make an appointment for the next day, others fidgeted with their cell phones and some of them distracted themselves by reprimanding their first-borns.

My mother was the first person I saw after speaking to Yusuf over the phone. As the tea brewed and as she fired questions at me, the tears ran down my cheeks. She is a tough, pragmatic woman and immediately started telling me stories of babies who were born with low birth weight and were thriving today. If I had a rand for every baby she knew who was brought home in a shoebox wrapped in cotton wool ... After saying everything a mother should say in the circumstances, she asked me what his current weight was: 580 grams. I was six months pregnant and looked about as pregnant as a marathon runner. She looked at the brick of Rama margarine in her hands and said nothing for a while. Occasionally, she encouraged me to finish my tea before it got cold. Now that I am a mother, I understand better the feeling of helplessness she must have been fighting. My tears would not stop. Someone had opened a tap and water kept pouring down into my lap. The tears were even starting to irritate me.

She watched me for a few minutes, then, in absolute panic, she shouted at me.

"This crying is making it much worse for the baby. You need to stop crying and get a hold of yourself. And you don't eat enough! You didn't even finish your tea."

She left the kitchen in a huff to attend to her own tears.

The next month was a precarious balance between waiting long enough for the foetus to be viable to live outside my womb as opposed to waiting too long and causing the baby to die in utero. I visited the gynaecologist daily to monitor my son's heartbeat and see if we could pull another 24 hours. Compounding the AIUGR, he was living in an environment of depleted amniotic fluid. On Sunday mornings, as spring set in, my gynaecologist would greet me warmly as he unlocked the door to his rooms, but I could tell that he was gravely concerned. Every day, there were these few seconds as he belted up my belly when he fell silent. I think he was pleading with God on my behalf. Eventually, dismissing the recommendations of two other specialists whom he had asked for second and third opinions, he told me that he was going to deliver the baby the next day.

"Why? We aren't at one kilogram yet!"

"Because you and I are going to die if I don't do this. I think he will be safer outside, it's what my gut is telling me."

He made perfect sense. For a month, my tears had not stopped. I had been incapable of having a conversation with an adult about anything without sobbing, but the emotion was purging and it was involuntary and there was nothing I could do about it.

My son was born at 6am, during a storm. Ordinarily, that is my favourite kind of weather, but this time it felt like a bad omen. We had prepared my older son for the inevitability of my not returning with a baby brother just yet and he seemed bored with the idea, asking if he could then get a dog instead. He was three, so he asked if the gynaecologist had not left yet to go pick up the delivery. No, he has not. Dad and I will go with him when its time.

The operating room was gloomy. I recalled the banter and the festive atmosphere of my previous childbirth on 15 December three years before. I remembered marvelling at the effectiveness of the spinal block, with my legs being moved about and me feeling nothing. I remembered how the gynae asked me if I could feel anything and I shouted "Yes! Stop! There's a mild tugging sensation," and he burst out laughing and said, "Wonderful! I have just cut through six layers of muscle." I remembered how I made my husband promise to describe to me everything he was seeing in gory detail. "Use adjectives", I told him and at some point he said, "OK Raz, it looks as though they have removed all your intestines, flipped them out and it's sort of on your chest but I could be wrong," as the colour drained from his face.

This time, nobody laughed. The nurses smiled at me and one of them held my hand and squeezed.

"You have an excellent team here, Mummy. It's going to be fine."

When they lifted him from me, he cried like a trouper and they rushed him away to the second set of specialists, leaving my gynaecologist and me alone. He stitched expertly, not wanting to pucker the skin, and tried to assure me of a bikini-worthy Caesarean scar. It was in vain. I had not seen my child. As soon as they put me in recovery, those blasted tears started again.

By the time my parents were allowed to visit, with Mikaeel, they had cried all their tears and were ready to face me. My mum burst into the room carrying pink roses, announcing that this child looked exactly like her. He does. My dad's contribution was that my son shares a birthday with Amitabh Bachchan, my childhood hero. He does. I pictured them preparing this script over a cup of tea in the morning. They compensated even more by visiting the canteen downstairs and buying my older son Mikaeel everything he asked for. I was sure that they had not insisted that he brush his teeth that morning and that they had allowed him to add three teaspoons of sugar to his tea. I did not ask how my baby was doing and them not offering any news was information enough. Nobody told me that his blood pressure kept crashing, his breathing was erratic and they were struggling to keep him alive. He had not made the one-kilogram weight we had been hoping for.

Almost two days after he was born, a nurse burst into the room and told me that my son was awake. Would I like her to wheel me to the Neonatal ICU? I declined the wheelchair, took a few deep breaths and followed her down the corridor. She pointed out his incubator and I wiped my tears; they were blurring my vision. I stood there for about three seconds before I fainted. I was expecting a very small baby. What I saw was miniscule: a naked, breathing, living foetus.

The nurses helped me into a wheelchair, irritated that I had declined the offer in the first place, and the matron bent down so that our heads were level. She was an impatient woman and her focus was on the well-being of the babies, not picking up wuss mothers who fainted.

"Listen here, Mummy. Your child is sick. We cannot have you coming here and crying and fainting and going on. This baby can feel your energy and you are going to be strong for him. Otherwise, stay out of Neonatal."

She instructed another nurse to wheel me back to my room. I could not get rid of the image of a small piece of clotted blood that had been stuck to his forehead. He looked like Gorbachev, bald and hairless. He had been sleeping with one hand under his chin, as I do. His newborn nappy started at just under his neck and ended just under his knees. His limbs were translucent, he was hairless and he was being fed formula through a tube into his stomach. They had literally cling-wrapped the incubator, the heater above him unable to generate enough warmth to compensate for his lack of body fat. He had a drip in his tiny wrist to supplement the formula, but he slept peacefully. His tongue had not developed a sucking reflex and I was told that, at the very least, he would need to stay until he could feed from breast or bottle. It was the bits of clotted blood that stuck to him that disturbed me the most. His skin was too fragile for a bath yet and so they had just wiped him down.

I was discharged on the same day that I saw him. I went home without a baby and appealed to my mum to ask people not to visit. Of course, people are bad at taking instructions so a few people trickled in, some with gifts and some without. I can imagine what a difficult call that must have been. Everyone had advice.

"You are being tested; your faith is being tested."

"What have you named him, names are important in Islam, it can pull him through. If he dies suddenly, he will need to have been named."

"NUK makes pacifiers for premature babies but you need to sign a disclaimer which gets sent to Germany in case he swallows it."

"Give eggs, bread and raw chickens away as an offering, it always works."

"Drink *badaam* milk, it will improve the quality of your breast milk and give him the nutrients he needs."

What nobody knew was that I had secretly decided that God could have him if He wanted him back. Wanting him to live *at any cost* was a deal that I had no right to conclude on his behalf.

The antidepressants had numbed my pain and the involuntary tears had stopped falling. It was going to be months before he would come home, if ever. Being able to drive to the hospital without tears blurring my vision was first prize for now. Three times a day, for three hours at a time, every day, for nine weeks.

I made the unilateral decision to name him Amaan. I loved the gentle way that the A and N landed at the end. Initially, I thought that it was a pretty-sounding name, but the Arabic meaning of the name, "to be divinely protected" was the confirmation that I needed. This child of mine was going to get every little advantage to thrive.

Our routine at home settled into a new normal. I would give Mikaeel breakfast, drop him off at nursery school and drive to the hospital. I would count the steps to the Neonatal ICU and greet all the people who had become so familiar to me. I had taken to bribing the nurses with tarts and roti and dropping off my offering for the day at the nurses' station before I settled into a chair to stare at my son. On some days, he would be crying when I got there, with nobody attending to him. On other days, he slept peacefully. I was not yet allowed to hold him; he was connected to too many tubes and I did not ask. Initially, as is the norm, his birth weight dropped and I would make sure I was present for the weigh-in every night as nurses changed shift. The theme song for *Rocky* would play in my head. The antidepressants had dulled the face I showed to the world, but I retained a semblance of my sense of humour. He was not gaining any weight at all and so I upped the offerings to the nurses, convinced that if they picked him up when he cried, he would conserve energy and not burn it all up. I replaced the standard Pick n Pay milk tarts with Black Forest cakes.

After Week Two I knew the politics of which paediatrician tried to duck being on call over the weekend and which paediatrician always stood in for him. The medical staff deconstructed my idea that doctors were rational and mature by bickering in the hallway as the timetable for the weekend was being negotiated. The weekend nurses mostly worked at public hospitals during the week and were moonlighting in private hospitals on weekends. As soon as I was told who would be in charge of my son, I would invite them to have some cake in the hope that they would change his nappy quickly enough to prevent a rash and soothe him when he cried that night. Highveld Stereo was the nurses' radio station of choice and even now I cannot hear Sean Kingston's "Beautiful Girls" without smelling the chemical hand sanitiser that had cut my hands to shreds and left them raw and bleeding.

Babies came and babies went. Families would assemble at the glass windows during visiting hours and the nurses would open the curtains and I would feel as though I was in a cage at the zoo. Not all the babies were ill; some were there for a few hours for observation before they were sent home. I would even smile when an older sibling's nose was pressed against the glass and she was shown the new baby, and Dad would lift his hand and wave, and Mummy, on the inside, would lift baby's hand and wave. When we brought Mikaeel to look through the glass, he was very disturbed and asked my husband if I had given birth to a rabbit. He never asked to see his brother again.

Strangely, the parents of the sick babies, all with a different long-term prognosis, did not chat and support each other. We would nod and acknowledge each other but that was it. Sometimes an incubator would be sterilised and the linen changed but I never asked if the baby had gone home or died. It made my reality more real and cemented for me just how little control I had over what was to come next. Amaan was by no means the sickest baby there. Inexplicably, babies with a higher birth weight and a far more hopeful prognosis would pass on in the middle of the night. Going back the next morning and noticing the empty incubator would have me picturing the mother sobbing with grief. In Neonatal, there was no distinction between day and night. The fluorescent lights shone mercilessly on the babies and it was noisy with the synthetic sounds of monitors and technology interspersed with Highveld Stereo. This glass coffin was not a world I would like to be born into.

There was a particular baby whose parents I remember well. They were an Afrikaans couple from the East Rand. I had not met the wife, but the husband visited the Neonatal ICU one morning to meet with the nurses. He was accompanied by the ob-gyn. When they left, the matron told me that the couple had had no idea what to expect when the baby was born. The ultrasound revealed severe congenital defects and physical abnormalities. Having lost seven babies at different stages of pregnancy in the last ten years, they were determined for this baby to live. In all likelihood, doctors would have to resuscitate and throw everything they had at keeping this baby alive.

"It's going to be a shit show, Razina. Maybe you don't want to be here. You can come back after four."

After five weeks of being together, the matron and I were practically sisters.

Just as I was preparing to leave at 2:30pm, the doors burst open and a team of nurses and doctors rushed to an incubator with this little baby. They were working furiously to keep him alive, the father watching, running his hands through his hair and pacing.

At some point, he shouted, "STOP! I need to speak to my wife," and ran out of the ward.

After ten minutes, he came back in. The team was standing around the baby, working slowly now, and he told them that he and his wife had decided not to resuscitate. Again, it is like a car accident that one drives past. You know that you should not look because once you have seen, you cannot unsee the carnage, but I looked over anyway. In the incubator was a full-term baby, with a stump as an arm and no legs. His head was severely deformed and his body was contorted into an abnormal position. He made a grunting sound, as if he were gasping for air but he did not cry once. Slowly, nurses started removing tubes and stepping away until only the father and paediatrician were left at the incubator. When the grunting stopped, the father threw himself into the doctor's arms and cried like I have never seen a grown man cry. When he composed himself, the paediatrician pointed out every single deformity and spoke about the mental challenges this child would have faced.

The father nodded silently and then left. "*Ek moet Sunette gaan sien* – I must go see Sunette."

I wanted to tell him that what I witnessed was one of the most brave decisions a parent could ever take, that I thought it was the right one, that life *at any cost* was selfish, but instead I turned my back on him and hoped that, in time, he would forgive himself.

Amaan's milestones were so delayed that although it is hard to imagine getting excited about cleaning an umbilical cord stump, we were over the moon when the nurse allowed my husband and me a go at it. She was distracted and tired and Highveld Stereo had played Rihanna's "Umbrella" five times during her shift and she had forgotten to bring her umbrella and she could knock off in ten minutes and collect her daughter from aftercare, if she could show us quickly how to do it before it started raining. She was holding the bottle of surgical spirits above his face, pouring some out, when his monitor beeped. She was startled and poured half the bottle into a coin-sized wad of cotton wool. It could not hold the liquid. The cold spirits poured into my son's eyes and I can only imagine the exquisite, searing pain on his paper-thin skin and in his open eyes. He pulled his legs up to his chest, all his blood vessels rose to his skin and he cried for an hour. We could not hold him and for the first time a tear threatened but the chemicals working on my brain did not allow it to fall. We decided not to report it; the nurse was back on shift in two days and the last thing I needed was for her to get into a disciplinary inquiry when it was she who would be changing my son's nappy and picking him up when he cried.

One night we received a call from the hospital at midnight asking for our permission to do an urgent, small procedure. It took us 15 minutes to get clothed and to drop Mikaeel off at my folks, and when we got there, the procedure had been done. There were tears on Amaan's face, but he was asleep. His chest had a new plaster and there were blood droplets showing through it. I grabbed a nurse and asked how they had managed to operate in such a short time, when they had given him the anaesthetic, who had gone with him to theatre and why this had been necessary. It turned out that his little wrists and ankles had "tissued" – they had swollen and the skin was tight and bruised – and so they needed a new site for the IV drip.

He was given Panado syrup and they cut him with a scalpel in his incubator.

Hearing that felt like an implosion in my body; my organs felt liquified at the thought of what that must have been like for him. As my heart hammered, I thought of how out of sync my face and my emotions had become. The pathways between my brain and my facial expression were blocked, and though I felt everything intensely, I knew my face was blank. I took some cotton wool and wiped my baby's tears. I asked Yusuf if he wanted a cup of coffee and asked him to remind me to send green chart-paper with Mikaeel to nursery school.

Praying, at this time, seemed like a very natural thing to do and I spoke to God all the time. It was not ritualistic prayer, but He became my confidant, in the way that you hold on to your new friend on the first day of school. I did not doubt that I was being heard, but I also knew that, however this turned out, it would be for the best. It is because of my love for my child that I wanted to spare him a lifetime of severe challenges. My bargaining with God was tempered by this ideological choice.

"It's Your call, so make a good one."

Of course, some family members misunderstood my chemical-fuelled haze as a particular religious position and they were convinced that, if they could get physically close enough to Amaan to pray, they could change the course of events. The concept of God being omnipresent did not occur to them. The Neonatal ICU is as sterile an environment as is humanly possible, with good reason. These babies are vulnerable to infection and nurses control the flow of people like a defence force. That did not stop a couple from convincing a nurse that they were my religious mentors and that I had given them permission to pray over my son. She practically bathed them in antiseptic and allowed them in. In their haste to be godly while breaking the rules and putting all the babies at risk they prayed at the wrong baby's incubator. Baby Du Plessis heard a long passage from the Quran and was blown on by my extended family. It was the first time I had laughed in five weeks.

Amaan was getting stronger and putting on weight. It was slow, but the upward trajectory had started and we finally put some clothes on him. He was swallowed up by the prem clothing, but I had the pride of a mother whose child was opening for a runway show. Another huge milestone was stopping the intravenous feeding, and I was allowed to hold the container of breast milk that fed the tube into his nose. Breastfeeding with panache. I had weaned myself off the antidepressants and, when I could see the light at the end of the tunnel, I allowed some emotion through.

Initially we could not generate any excitement in

Mikaeel. His brother was that promised puppy that never materialised. I had braced myself for fantastic tantrums from Mikaeel, who had been very attached to me, for not having me around as much, but I was wrong. His level of understanding made no sense to us; he was only three. It could have been the sugary tea he grew accustomed to at my mum's house that took the edge off the separation anxiety. Or perhaps it was the many visits to the hospital canteen that made this a situation he could easily live with.

We brought Amaan home at the end of December 2007. He weighed two kilograms. Within a month, his cheeks filled out like two plump apples and he started smiling at his brother, who now chattered at him non-stop. I became unpopular with my extended family, often greeting guests at the door and stalling them while signalling to my husband to whisk Amaan into a different room to prevent infection. Physically, he thrived. He fed easily, he slept easily and he rarely cried. Within three months of arriving home, he looked like one of Raphael's cherubs.

We were warned of developmental lags – in fact, we were told to expect them. We would calculate backwards to his birthdate and he seemed on track, but for the AIUGR. There was one thing that worried me. Amaan made very few sounds. Apart from the giggles he would share with his brother, he made no gurgling sounds. Nothing. Sometimes I would take something away from him, hoping to invoke a squeal, but he would hand it over readily and not seem upset. I stopped doing that when it started feeling cruel. When he wanted something, he would sometimes point at it. I stopped passing him things he pointed to, but he seemed happy to live without them. When I confided in my mum, she asked if, between Mikaeel and me, anyone could get a word in edgewise. I was apparently a very chatty child and Mikaeel was the same and she took some pleasure in watching me squirm every time he asked, "But why…". In an ideal world we all have the time and patience to answer these questions, but after the eleventh time I would say "because the sky is so high". Like a good mother should.

Mikaeel spoke to my husband and me non-stop, he asked questions, he offered his opinion, often loudly, and he hated being uncomfortable.

I had to stop Mikaeel from putting Amaan in a small plastic laundry basket and sliding him across the floors in our home because although he did not protest, he looked terrified. He would hold his neck stiff and pull his knees up to his chest, holding on to the edges of the basket.

"But he doesn't miiiinnnndd, Mum!" Mikaeel would argue.

"Yes, he does, look at his face."

Amaan was three and a half, it was midwinter, and my husband was heading out to Checkers to fill the grocery list I had finished writing. Mikaeel bounced into the room and asked if he could go with "for a drive" but he knew that the odds of Dad buying sweets were much higher than if he went with me. Yusuf and I understood that Amaan would stay home. The previous year he had had bronchial pneumonia and a short hospital stay which made us extra vigilant in keeping him home and away from the shops.

"Buy sweets for Amaan also – he likes those purple Rascals packets," I said to Mikaeel as Yusuf slid a beanie onto his head. He was six years old with a wicked sense of humour and so he feigned surprise that I was endorsing his intentions.

"Really? I can have sweets?"

As they were leaving, Amaan stood up. "Can Amaan please come with to Checkers? He doesn't like those Rascals sweets Dad keeps buying for him. He can choose his own sweets."

All three of us stopped moving. We stared at him in stunned silence. His tone and pronunciation of each word far surpassed his age. He sounded exactly like me, with a child's voice.

"Amaan will go put a beanie on his head." And with that, he went in search of a hat.

Chapter 19

Fig Trees and Restless Geriatrics

Everything about the house was perfect. After 18 months of searching for a home my husband and I had found something which we believed was good value for money in a neighbourhood we had fallen in love with. In fairness, the house was a little big for my small family, but when last have you heard a buyer ask if they could have the same house with fewer bedrooms and bathrooms for the same price?

It is an old home with parquet floors and lots of natural sun, and magnificent jacaranda trees line the pavement on my property boundary. After eight years of living here, the novelty of them in full bloom has not worn off, to the extent that I instructed our gardener never to rake the lilac flowers from the ground until they were dark brown or the threat of bees creating a hive was imminent. William Njiko, the gardener, was disgusted at this request. He asked for clarity five times and then shook his head in shame when I paid him. I could sense his anguish at leaving the ground strewn with the flowers: he is a perfectionist. Once, returning from the December break, he walked into my garden and had a heated argument with my husband and me about our not watering the plants. We explained patiently that there were water restrictions in place, but William was beside himself, walking from plant to plant and muttering apologies to them, lifting his hands to the sky occasionally while giving my husband and me disgusted glances. He would arrive at 8am fortnightly, and having hidden away the hose pipe, we would avoid him. It was eventually a tropical storm called Dineo that saved our relationship with William.

There were two things that bothered me about this home. The estate agent had mentioned that the owner, a widow, had her geriatric parents living with her until their death. Their bathroom had been modified with support handles in the shower and on either side of the toilet. At no point did my husband or I ask whether they had died in this very house. He, because he knows me so well, and I, because I know myself so well.

The other minor concern was the fig tree in my garden. In winter the tree sheds its peculiarly shaped leaves and only the branches remain. When the moon rises in the background, it is an eerie sight. It looks like the skeleton of a geriatric.

The week we moved in, friends and family commented on every aspect of our home, sharing our excitement and making all the appropriate sounds.

Fig Trees and Restless Geriatrics

"You have a stoep? You can braai here in summer."

"You have a fireplace? You are going to love sitting in the lounge in winter."

"You have steel kitchen units? They don't make them this strong anymore."

And then: "You have a fig tree." That was always a statement. Depending on the time of day, guests either backed off slowly or had an expression that said, "Rather you than me."

The tree started to bother me. I found myself staring at it in the moonlit garden from the lounge. I can't say what I was hoping to see. It was what I could not see that worried me.

Hesitantly, I shared my concerns with my husband, not quite knowing how to broach the subject as he couldn't wait for the first figs of the season to appear.

"Are you serious?" He knows I hate him to ask that question. Different friends have different triggers. A friend of mine hates her husband to tell her to "relax" when he should know that she has considered that option, toyed with the idea, rejected the idea of "relaxing" as being inappropriate in the circumstances and is about to have an enormous breakdown.

He could tell that I was indeed serious and expected him to do something about it. While I was silently hoping he would concede and call a tree-felling company, he marched outside and stood under the fig tree at sunset – for dramatic effect – and announced that we had, in fact, paid a lot for this house and if there was "anybody" living here rent free, they should please find other premises because he didn't recall welcoming tenants from any realm. He thought that his show and tell was hilarious, but I was mortified. By this point, I had convinced myself that there was something, well, untoward, about the tree and his flippant attitude made me even more determined to have it removed.

My sons, who were six and three when we moved in, were terrified in this new home. I consider myself a rational and scientific person and I put their unease down to the fact that, in our previous home, we could all see each other no matter where we were in the house. This home had actual rooms and the boys were simply not used to the space. After sunset, especially if my husband was not home, they would walk behind me wherever I went, and if I stopped suddenly, they would bump into me. They became my shadows, often scaring me if I turned suddenly to find two sets of wide-eyed Lilliputians looking at me. How shall I say this? I was *poep-bang*.

My older son's nights became restless and he would often call for my husband and me. "Muuuuuum, Daaaaaaad," and when we entered the room, "I'm scared".

On the nights when my husband was working, I was tempted to say, "Shit, I'm scared too," but I went through the motions of checking under his bed, ruffling the curtains and praying quietly with him, all the while trying to still my hammering heart. The trusses in the ceiling would creak as the house lost heat and I would feel torn between being grateful that it kept them awake as I would then be occupied with implausible scientific explanations, and hoping they would sleep so that I could investigate the sounds to appease my own sceptical mind.

Fig Trees and Restless Geriatrics

About a month after we had moved in, I woke up one morning to find my sons had slept through the night. Throwing the blankets aside, I ran into their room, half expecting to see them levitating above their beds with the windows wide open, the curtains blowing in the wind. Instead, they were sleeping.

I got back into bed, thinking that the exhaustion of the move was making me delusional. My older son bounced into the room and squeezed himself between my husband and me.

"Well done, my angel! You see? Nothing to be scared of at all! I'm so proud of you!"

"You're right, Mum! The auntie even came last night and stood by my bed."

He noticed I was silent and elaborated.

"I opened my eyes and she was just looking at me. I was about to say, "Muuuuuum" and she did this ..." He lifted his fingers to his lips, shook his head from side to side.

"And then she told me not to be scared and to tell you not to be scared, because everyone who lives here is always happy. And she thinks you are VERY scared. She was very kind, very."

My husband sat right up. "Are you serious?"

I felt vindicated, relieved that he had witnessed this creepy exchange and would be obliged to react.

My son ignored the question and bounced out of the room to wake his sleeping brother.

"You heard the woman," my husband said to me, "Don't be scared." He adjusted his pillows and went back to sleep.

I am the product of generations who would scream, "Get

into the house! It's *Maghrib* time!" In summer, just as the jasmine tree in the Yard would release its powerful perfume at sunset, children would be coaxed into ending their games and encouraged to get back to the safety of the flat. It was only considered safe to play outside again once all light in the sky had disappeared and men had returned from the mosque.

I never knew exactly what would happen if we continued to play around the tree at sunset, but the adults alluded to jinns and exorcism. There were few rules set in stone, but this was one of them. Even the Hindu children we played with complied, so I have never been sure whether the link between demonic possession and trees is rooted in Islam or Hinduism, or if it is just an import from the Indian sub-continent.

But I was convinced the fig tree and the old lady in the house were linked.

Sometimes, according to my aunties, the passing smell of camphor or eucalyptus predicts a death in the family of the person who smelt it. Deceased bodies were fragranced with camphor before Muslim burials, making the smell of camphor synonymous with death. I have never bought into this superstition for two reasons: firstly, men never got passing smells of anything, and secondly, the women in my family would only smell camphor when they were with each other.

"Do you smell that?"

"What are you smelling?"

Both would sniff the air for dramatic effect. The first auntie would lower her voice and then, "Camphor or something."

Fig Trees and Restless Geriatrics

"No man! I am not smelling anything! You are always smelling these things!"

The second auntie's sole purpose in this interaction was to convince the first auntie that she was imagining the smell. If there was a death in the family within six months of this exchange, both aunties would claim to have seen it coming. This superstition is rare these days and I suspect it is because Ingram's Camphor Cream has made way for more pleasant-smelling moisturising options.

But now my lack of interest in the world of superstition was redundant. Something about the early years of twilight cautions from the Yard in Vorster Street had stuck. Because whenever I applied Pascal's Wager to the probability of the fig tree housing a jinn I came down firmly on the side of the believers. By my reckoning, the fig tree had to go and the souls of the restless couple should be relocated. I bought incense sticks and planned a cleansing ceremony.

It might also have been my traumatic viewing, aged five, of *The Exorcist* that had me trying to convince my husband that the jinns were attempting to contact the children and it would be only days before one of our kids did a backwards spider crawl down Orange Road.

"They would have to be very fit to pull that off," was his response.

I was in the kitchen of my home when the ground under my feet shook feverishly followed by a sound as of a train wreck and then absolute stillness. The sound had come from outside and I ran towards the lounge to get the best view of what was clearly a catastrophe. It is impossible to say what I thought it could be; suffice to say that stories of the Second Coming of Christ were at the forefront of my racing mind.

Then, like a person running at full speed about to paraglide off a cliff and then having second thoughts, my feet braked. Bricks and chunks of cement lay smoking on the ground. Electric fence alarms were screaming in protest at wires being dislodged and ripped. Seventy-seven metres of boundary wall around my property had collapsed.

My home felt naked and exposed to the outside world. Fleetingly, I thought that my mother was correct, curtains are an integral part of any home. I had none. Bless my friend Tahira, who could easily have stepped over a few bricks: she walked stoically to where the entrance would have been and used the non-existent gate to soften the blow.

Neighbours and friends commiserated and everybody reassured us that the insurance company would honour the claim as there was nothing we could do in the face of an Act of God. Insurers define an Act of God as any accident or event that is not influenced by man. I like that phrase; it takes human error out of the equation while justifying the premiums that insurance companies charge.

The assessor stepped into my garden the following day. Friendly and warm, he and I estimated the cost of erecting a new wall to be upwards of R100 000. I treated him like a Messiah and he gave me every indication that the claim would be settled in full. To be sure, I fried samoosas, thinking that one can never be too sure. I loathe stereotypes but not as much as I loathed the idea of forking out that amount of money.

His response, via email, was as follows:

Dear Ms Theba,
I regret to inform you that XYZ company has repudiated your claim for the erection of a boundary wall at your property situated on the corner of Orange and Bhira Streets, Emmarentia.

After thorough investigation, we have concluded that the destruction was caused by the invasive roots of the *Ficus carica* plant, commonly known as the fig tree. Maintenance of trees and damage caused by trees is exclusively for the account of the property holder.

Regards,
Mr John Black

Suddenly, the curse of the fig tree made sense. I imagine houses in Indian villages crumbling near fig trees, collapsing like dominoes in the vicinity of the invasive roots. The innocuous, lively green leaves of the fig tree hide Medusa's root system.

My reply to the assessor was as follows:

Dear Mr Black,
Thank you for your speedy response. I saw this Act of God coming.
Regards,
Razina Theba

Chapter 20

My Dermatologist, the Psychologist

"Theba?"

I stood up, grabbed my handbag and slung it over my shoulder.

"Not you," the dermatologist told me, looking slightly fed up, "Theba."

"That's me," I said as I passed through the glass door.

"Oh. I was expecting someone else," he mumbled as he walked into the consulting room ahead of me.

I am used to this. By pure coincidence, my surname is shared by a genus of air-breathing land snails in the Canary Islands called *Theba pisana* and it is also a common Zulu surname in South Africa.

My sister, who is the storyteller of our family, created an entire fake family of Zulu relatives and ancestors in

My Dermatologist, the Psychologist

KwaZulu-Natal. I need to keep reprimanding her when she tells her colleagues that somebody has died in our family and so she must attend the "after-tears" party. She uses the smattering of isiZulu that she does know liberally and audaciously and I find myself disengaging slowly when anyone enquires about our surname and she announces that it is *such* an interesting story.

When asked, my dad proudly proclaims that it is an Indian surname from India originating from Bharuch district, specifically the village of Tankaria, in Gujarat Province, and even more specifically, near the seaport where the river bends, the heart of commercial trade in Gujarat Province and where there are flushing toilets. My dad has never visited India, but he could not be prouder of his heritage.

Prior to 1994, I had not given my surname much thought, having been raised in an insular society entirely surrounded by individuals of Indian heritage. Besides, all my cousins on my father's side shared the surname. My dad's side of the family is huge. He had nine siblings and I have 40 first cousins.

The strangeness of my surname became apparent when I was pulled over by a traffic officer soon after apartheid ended. New to driving, the only crime I could have committed was driving too slowly and too carefully.

"Who is this?" The traffic officer looked at my picture. "It is not you."

I frowned at him through the driver's window. The sun was setting behind him. I could see him salivating at the prospect of a bribe.

"It is me," I told him.

"No. You are not Theba."
What do I say to that?
"I am."
"Is it your father or your husband who is black?"

This was the response I received from our Metro law-enforcement officers after I had produced my green ID document, my bank cards and my student card, and he had radioed the traffic department for confirmation.

"Neither," I told him as I drove off, feeling very self-righteous that I chose not to save myself half an hour by parting with the R20 in my wallet. I was not about to pay someone to believe that I was me.

By 1997, the last year of my undergraduate degree at Wits, the novelty of my surname had worn thin and I started spelling it for receptionists as "Themba without the M". It made more sense, it saved time and everyone understood the first time. I would bang my student card on the counter to save them having to ask for confirmation. The invigilators in exams were the worst, standing over me, looking more confused than the first years as their eyes darted between me and my student card. Friends confirmed that they hardly noticed the invigilators; it was I who alleviated their boredom in Hall 29 during a three-hour paper.

As the years went by, South Africans grappled with labels and identities and emerged unfazed by a white South African Dlamini and a black South African Coetzee. We learnt our new national anthem with enthusiasm and sang it with vigour and started embracing our differences, superficially at least. What a feast for advertising agencies! There was no dearth of advertisements on TV demonstrating the

My Dermatologist, the Psychologist

Rainbow Nation hugging, socialising and bonding. My poor husband was teased relentlessly on the eve of our wedding thanks to the Spekko rice advertisement whose jingle title was Margaret Singana singing "Mama Thembu's getting married here tonight".

I have had my fair share of hilarity about my surname, but nothing came close to my graduation. In fairness, we arts graduates are a happy bunch. Three years of analysis, engaging and critique and, in my case, a year of reading Geoffrey Chaucer out loud in 14th century medieval English ensured that the graduation was going to be a good *jol*. It was well-deserved. After writing an arts exam, you never know whether you have achieved a first or failed. There are never straightforward answers, which makes the graduation even more rewarding. I cannot imagine that the commerce graduations are half as much fun.

So, there we were, all the graduates, sitting in alphabetical order and patiently waiting our turn. As you walked on stage, there was a "primer". He probably has a specific name, but his job was to smile and send you on your way as your name was called. He ensured that the person corresponded with the name being called. This special person reminded me of the women who guide the actors on stage during the Oscars. They serve no real purpose because it is very unlikely that one would send an imposter to receive a scroll or would get lost on a stage.

With every name being called, I started noticing a pattern from the audience.

"Bhengani!" Rapturous, wild, generous applause and ululating.

"Cebekhulu!" Rapturous, wild, generous applause and ululating.

"Dlamini!" Rapturous, wild, generous applause and ululating.

"Dawson!" Polite and constrained applause from the two family members who attended.

"Dladla!" Rapturous, wild, generous applause and ululating.

"Edwards!" Polite and constrained applause from the two family members who attended.

My heart was hammering away, thinking that I had three seconds to convince Mr Primer to allow me to walk across that stage. I am who I say I am.

"Theba!" Rapturous, wild generous applause and ululating until I walked across the stage. Midway through, the applause died. Flat. Confusion reigned supreme in those two seconds. One could not even hear the polite constrained claps from my parents. And then, the confusion of the traffic officer, the invigilators and my dermatologist gave way to the spirit of Kumbaya, Ubuntu, our Rainbow Nation and the audience rose as one to say, "Whatever the back-story is, we don't care, you have an arts degree, congratulations!" and went wild.

This was more than two decades ago, which was why the dermatologist's remark that he was "expecting someone else" caught me by surprise. It had been a long time since I had to respond to such intrusive remarks and deal with preconceptions about skin tone and surname fitting together like a puzzle in a preconceived box.

And it should have prepared me for what was to come.

My Dermatologist, the Psychologist

We settled down in his plush office and he took a questionnaire from a pile sitting squarely in the middle of his desk.

The elderly dermatologist had a weary look on his face, the expression of someone who had spent decades treating patients. He did not have the cheery disposition of a newly qualified specialist. He had solved so many medical problems he now barely bothered with bedside manner.

He started. "Where are you from?"

I did not answer. Did he mean like five minutes ago, where do I live, where was I raised, where do I now live? The possibilities were endless.

I answered, "From where ... like where do I live?"

"No man. I mean are you Gujarati?"

By then, in my head, he was not a professor whom I had come to consult with. He was, firstly, an uncle who recognised me as coming from the same cultural grouping as his and no matter what my level of education, my area of expertise, my sex, my class or my problem, he was going to remove any filters he may have had and just relate to me as though I was his niece. He would take time to enquire about my family and the well-being of my children. It is done to establish a *connection*, like a kinsmanship. When it is done in the context of a service being offered, like my dermatologist, it never affects the quality of care or expertise no matter what one's answer is.

In Western cultures, professionalism is prioritised. In Indian culture, we defer to age unless the interaction is deeply unsettling. Older people will think nothing of asking how much you earn, how many children you plan on having and what your toddler plans on studying. I suspect that it is used to establish rapport with no ill intention.

"Right. How old are you, Theba? Theba. Am I saying it right? You sure Gujarat Province?"

"Well no ... more like Emmarentia. I haven't been to India."

He did not look at me, not even fleetingly. The questionnaire was suddenly particularly important, and both he and I focused on the document that was going to justify my vanity.

"I'm 44," I replied.

"And how long have you been 44 for?" Deadpan and monotone.

I paused and looked at his face, tempted to answer but giving him the benefit of the doubt for a second.

"Hehehe, clever. Most of my patients try to answer that one. Spring chicken," he said to himself, still sniggering.

"OK, Theba, let us get through these questions before I examine your skin. It's not rocket science; you should get through easily."

What? I reminded myself, this should take ten minutes, in and out, get the script and move along.

Dermatologist: How many hours do you spend in the sun every day?

Me: Hours? No, I'm rarely in the sun, maybe 15 minutes a day, as I'm driving or ...

Dermatologist: What's your diet like? Coke, chocolates ...

Me: Hardly, if ever.

Dermatologist: Do you eat lots of oily things, achaar, chutneys?

My Dermatologist, the Psychologist

Me: Never.

Dermatologist: (*Looking directly at me, leaning forward with shock on his face*) Not even with biryani? Not on Eid day? Not with a fresh loaf of naan?

Me: *No, Sam I am, not in a house, not in a box, not on a tree* ... Instead, I say, No, never.

Dermatologist: What the hell do you do for fun? Never mind, don't answer that. Somehow, I don't think the answer will be very inspiring.

I was stupefied. Mortified and stunned. It was the correct doctor. I had googled him before the consultation, his face matched the person sitting opposite me. Not only was he experienced but he held the highest academic position possible. This was not an imposter. He wrote articles that were peer-reviewed, for goodness sake. His article in the *South African Medical Journal* about the steep rise in facial warts and fungal infections being a probable result of hairdressers not washing their hands did the rounds on social media for weeks. Almost every Pakistani, Bangladeshi and Indian hairdresser had read the article. He may have changed hygiene practice in their salons forever.

The day I saw him, all of this was difficult to believe.

Dermatologist: How long have you had acne for?

Me: Two months.

Dermatologist: Shame, you poor thing!

It was at this point that my friends say that they would have walked out. I cannot say what kept me in that chair: being treated this way did not suit my assertive personality. Something in my gut told me to be patient, this was building up to something, there was a point to this madness. I kept looking around for hidden cameras. If this was a set-up in a reality show, I was onto it.

We walked into a brightly lit room and he arranged his equipment in preparation for examining my skin. He worked slowly and deliberately and I thought to myself, *Finally! He is doing his job.* The quips were relentless, though.

"Theba, do you have your master's?"

"No, I have children," I said, trying to lie still as a needle hovered over my eye, hoping this would end soon.

Wrong answer. He stepped back. "So is that an excuse?"

It took every ounce of discipline for me not to grab the needle from his gloved hands and stab him in the chest with it. Instead, I said, "It's complicated."

The examination itself took less than two minutes. I was told that I have beautiful skin, *mashallah*. My skin was somewhat dry but nothing serious. He counted three pimples, which, he said, had more than likely made an appearance due to stress. He pointed at them with a needle whose sole purpose was to inject cystic acne. I didn't have acne and therefore there was no need to inject me.

He walked back into the consulting room, leaving me lying on the bed. He had made his pronouncement: it was stress.

WHAT! Was that it? By then, because my personality had been trampled on for the last half an hour and I had endured all his insults, I made a monumental mistake. My law lecturers would have been so disappointed. I asked a question I did not know the answer to.

"Can you tell me something I don't know?" I mumbled. Again, I deferred to his age. You want to dish it out, you must

My Dermatologist, the Psychologist

be willing to taste your own medicine, or some cliché like that.

I wanted a script, I wanted ointments, I wanted a list of beauty products I could buy, I did not want pimples after forty, dammit.

He seemed amused at my newfound voice.

"Sit, Theba ... You know, your surname is really weird. I have never heard it before." He pointed at the chair opposite him. "Sit, I have a few minutes. And I like you. Don't ask me why ..."

URRGHHH!!!

"So, I grew up poor, like *dirt poor*, and you will not even begin to imagine what that feels like. With lots of luck and some hard work, I became a doctor. Of course, my parents were very proud."

That goes without saying, I thought to myself.

"Let me tell you what justifies stress. Losing a child justifies stress. Sometimes having a child with a mental illness is horribly stressful. Not being able enough to feed your family while working like a dog is a constant stress. Having everything you could want and then being diagnosed with cancer or an auto-immune disease is another stress. Having your children walk ten kilometres a day to school and then knowing that they are using a pit latrine. That is stressful. Not having enough money to send your teenager to university. Stressful. Widowed at a young age ..."

He went on.

"Coming to see me feels like you are wasting your time. You seem healthy, you are a lawyer, you people make *big money* I hear, you have two healthy children ... did you choose your own husband?"

That one took me by surprise.

"The things that stress you out are ..." He struggled for a word and then it came. "*Self-indulgent.*"

"Go do your master's, Theba. Your children are going to grow up despite you trying to make them a better version of yourself. Their destiny is written. The school you are sending them to is an exceptionally good school, my boys went there. And one is a *doctor.*"

I had to smile at his last remark.

"DRINK LIFE, Theba. Drink it because by the time you realise how short it is, it will be too late."

"So, I will give you a script. But know this: if I could get you to stop stressing, you would not need a script. I am treating the manifestation, not the underlying cause. I will leave you to figure that one out."

He walked me out, but not without a final quip. "Do you know that the study of psychology is bullshit? I won't be charging you for the advice. Now I need to see some people with real problems."

Of course, he was right. Psychologists have told me never to allow anybody to minimise my stress. My stress is my stress. On that day, it took an Indian uncle, my weird surname and an excuse for us to meet for a monumental shift in priorities.

Epilogue

By Day 10 of the lockdown, the stillness of each day had me thinking about who each of us is and the ways in which we are different. The previous week, I had been cutting potatoes to make chips while my younger son tried to convince me that it was perfectly ethical to take a photo of a model that his brother had built three years earlier and pass it off as his own work. I had been at my wits' end because he would not back down.

Finally I said, "Because right is right!"

"That makes no sense, Mum."

But he walked away defeated, knowing that those words were my final answer. He had heard me use them before, sparingly, lovingly, but I do not reach for them too easily because the history and weight of those words are beyond his years. I hope one day he will reach for them too.

The next day I unwrapped the beige high heels that I had bought before lockdown and wore them with jeans and a T-shirt all day and answered "Nowhere" thrice as members of my family noticed my footwear. Time passes, seasons change, the world as we knew it may never return, red velvet coats stop fitting and so I wore my beige high heels in my home and went nowhere.

If Amaan asked me now whether anyone will remember him when he dies, I have an answer. This collection of vignettes, reflections on my experiences and growth with the assortment of characters who have been a part of my life for 45 years, is part of it. It is a long, complicated answer, I know. Because by osmosis and with no warning, we absorb the idiosyncrasies and truths and lessons of people we have met.

And we in turn become a part of the lives of others. We transform and are transformed by each other. We turn hopeless situations into something new.

In the final days of writing this book, I went back to the Yard. I had not been back in 25 years. As I left to go to Fordsburg, I thought briefly to take something with me. Something to hold in my hand to make my presence less pointless. Eventually I told myself that I was being silly. I would leave before I was noticed.

As I drove up the narrow entrance to the Yard, the first thing that struck me was that the driveway had been paved. Custom had taught me to park on the right, close to the wall and away from the flats. I recognised the perennial jasmine tree to my left. I parked my car, stepped out and took in the

Epilogue

scene around me. It was late in the afternoon and the smell of frying onions hung in the air.

There was a group of six children, five boys and a girl, playing cricket. The children wore no protective equipment, used a tennis ball instead of a cricket ball and were using a big black bin as stumps. The sound the hollow bin made would settle the inevitable argument about whether or not the batter was out.

On the washing lines hung rows of white *kurtas* of different sizes and a few colourful *punjabis*. The children had noticed me but continued their game. I was leaning against my car, too close for them to huddle together in conference with each other about my presence. I told myself I would leave when the little girl had finished batting.

A woman in her thirties left her flat and walked slowly towards the row of bins on the far side of the Yard. She deposited a small piece of newspaper there and walked back even more slowly, hardly taking her eyes off me. I got the message. *These children are being supervised.*

I thought to myself that I had a few more minutes before my standing there watching the children would feel weird, even to me. The bowler asked his fielders to move back, gesturing wildly as the female batter resumed her position. She took her scarf, which had been loosely flung across her body shoulder to shoulder, and tied it around her waist. She was the youngest of the lot, but with the most determined look on her face.

The kids spoke to each other in perfect Gujarati, children of first-generation Gujarati immigrants, the Gujarati my mum and her siblings spoke.

The bowler took a ridiculously long run-up and flung the tennis ball. One would have to be a block away not to hear the hollow thud. The fielders and bowler began celebrating by yelling "Out!" and running towards each other. At the same time, the loudest, most protest-worthy voice was the female batter, "NOOO BAAALLL!"

That settled any argument and every child moved back into position.

Just then, the same woman who had walked to the bins screamed to her son from her flat window, "ISHHAAAQ! MAGHRIB!" Only, it wasn't *Maghrib* time. My presence had unsettled her and this was a reminder to me that I was a pariah and it was time for me to move along.

I got back into my car and left the Yard.

Everyone has a place that holds the past in its hand ... for me that is the home on Vorster Street. Even so, I made the decision never to return. These memories are mine but I am ready to relinquish the space to those children.

Glossary

aara – Lookout

achaar – Indian-type pickle made from vegetables and fruit. Often preserved in vinegar and oil.

adoo masala – Ginger, garlic and chilli paste which forms the base of most Indian cooking

adoo-pak – Ginger and almond pulp

after-tears – South Africanism for a gathering after a funeral

ahre ahre – Without measurement. An estimation of quantity.

Allah hafiz – May God be your guardian. Used at the end of a meeting or before travelling.

apa – Respectful term for Muslim female teacher

Asr – Third compulsory prayer of the day for Muslims, often performed mid-afternoon

As-salamu alaykum – May peace be with you. Universal Muslim greeting.

badaam – Almond

bajee – Generic term for grandfather in Gujarati

bajia – Deep-fried spicy Indian snack made from lentil flour

barfee – Sweet, rich Indian delicacy made with condensed milk, cashews, pistachios, almonds and clarified butter

bhai – Literally, brother. Often preceded by the person's name.

Bharuch – City in India. The lazy British tongue called it Broach.

bhen – Literally, sister. Often preceded by the person's name.

bhiroo – A wrap with a filling of meat, vegetable and/or potato

bimri rice – A type of jasmine rice. It is as fragrant as basmati rice but cheaper and more sticky once boiled.

biryani – A rice dish with vegetables, spices, meat, yoghurt, sour milk, lentils, garlic and clarified butter. Popular in India and having a reputation for being an expensive dish to prepare, many countries lay claim to its origin.

boula – Brazier

burka – In other parts of the world, a veil that covers the entire body and face, but in the South African context, a covering that covers a female's hair and forms a loose-fitting garment down to her waist

cha-cha – Generic Indian term for uncle

chai – Literally, tea, but specifically a tea infused with cardamon, cinnamon and ginger and boiled on a stove top. Do not ever ask for chai-tea.

Glossary

champals – Slip-slop type of footwear

compos mentis – Having full control of one's mind (Latin)

coolie – Historically used to describe an unskilled Asian or Chinese labourer but used disparagingly in South Africa to describe a person of Indian heritage.

daadi – Paternal grandmother

dhai – Spiced sour milk or yoghurt accompaniment to rice dishes

dhania – Coriander seeds or leaves

dik – Literally, thick, but often used in Afrikaans to indicate fed up

dolus eventualis – Legal intention (Latin)

driehoek koelie-koek – Literally, three-cornered coolie cake. Derogatory description of a deep-fried Indian snack such as a samoosa.

dua – Prayer

Eid – One of two religious holidays in Islam

Eneh noh chere – Do not provoke him (Gujarati)

Fajr salah – First compulsory Muslim prayer of the day, performed before sunrise.

foi – Father's sister. Preceded by the person's name

gatvol – Fed up or annoyed (Afrikaans)

ghee – Clarified butter

ghusal – Bathing of deceased body before burial according to Muslim rites

godroos – Weighted blanket or heavy duvet

gorimummy – Generic term for one's maternal uncle's wife

Haai sies – Afrikaans slang to show disgust

halaal – Arabic word meaning permissible or lawful

haram – Arabic word

237

meaning unlawful, forbidden
hidayat – Arabic word meaning instruction. Often used to indicate good advice or good counsel.
hiddoh – Literally, to straighten. Used in Gujarati more colloquially to indicate a person who has learnt a lesson.
Hy is 'n groot cleva – He is a "big clever", as in streetwise or a city-slicker (Afrikaans)
ijaars – Pants/trousers
impimpi – a police informant or a spy
Isha – Fifth compulsory Muslim prayer of the day, usually performed in the early part of the evening.
issab-kitaab – Checks and balances
izzat – Integrity, honour or pride
jaan – Life
jajroo – Toilet
jaldi – Quickly

JazakAllah – May you be blessed. Often used instead of "thank you".
Jee pooirie – Yes, child
jinn – Spirit from another realm
jol – Party (Afrikaans)
jungli – From the Indian jungle. Uncouth, wild.
kabr – Grave
Ka che? – Where is?
Kanamia – People from Bharuch district in India
kari-kitchri – Indian rice and sour milk dish
khatam – Recitations of the Quran; also, to complete a task
Ketloo roopari! – How pretty!
khala – Generic term for one's mother's sister. Often preceded by the person's name.
klap – Smack (Afrikaans)
koelie – Afrikaans for 'coolie'
kumbaya – Used to describe a situation that is overly optimistic, from

Glossary

the religious song of the name
kurta – Loose collarless shirt
Kyk, die koelie-baba slaap! – Look, the "coolie" baby is sleeping!
Kyk, Pa, kyk! – Look, Dad, look!
laatlammetjie – Literally, a late lamb in Afrikaans. Often used to describe a child born to elderly parents.
ma – Mother or grandmother. My name for my grandmother.
madressa – Muslim religious school
Maghrib – Third compulsory Muslim prayer of the day, performed just after sunset
Mashallah – Allah has willed
mashwara – Consultative meeting
maulana – Learned Muslim scholar

mehndi – Henna
mithi paan – Sweetened betel nut leaf snack
motima – Elder aunt
Motti pooirie – Eldest daughter
muezzin – Man who calls Muslims to prayers from the minaret of a mosque
muti – Traditional African medicine or magical charms
naan – Leavened and unleavened flatbread
naani – Maternal grandmother
Nasara – People of Nazareth/Christians
nazms – Genre of Urdu poetry, often exalting God
nê – Colloquial, adding a tone of enquiry in speech (Afrikaans)
nikah – Islamic marriage contract/ the marriage
niqab – A veil covering the face, hair and body. Worn by some Muslim women.
Oo taneh mara – I will hit you.

ouma – Grandmother (Afrikaans)
paan – Betel nut leaf. Often wrapped with spices and nuts.
paan dabbo – Betel nut container
paan walla – Seller of betel nut leaf snack
paapar – Poppadum, crispy deep-fried bread, served with rice dishes
padkos – Literally, road-food (Afrikaans)
pap – Soggy (Afrikaans)
pareloo paani – Holy water
Piet-my-vrou – Red-chested cuckoo bird. Named after its call.
poep-bang – Slang. Very scared (Afrikaans).
pooirie – Daughter/girl
pooirie waaste – For the daughter/girl
poori (also Puri): a deep-fried piece of bread made of unleavened wheat flour.
punjabis – Traditional dress of women in the Punjab region. The *punjabi* consists of three parts – a long shirt-type dress, loose pants and a scarf.
pur – Thin, crispy pastry. Often used to encase a filling and then deep fried.
Quls – Short prayers in the Holy Quran recited for protection
Quran – Islamic sacred book
rag – University-run charity organisation
roti – Soft, flat, unleavened bread
Salaat – A prescribed liturgy performed five times a day. The second pillar of Islam.
samoosa – Deep-fried triangular Indian pastry. Often filled with meat, vegetables or lentils.
saumph – Fennel seeds
sawab – Blessings/heavenly rewards
skottel – Dish (Afrikaans)
slap chips – Deep-fried

Glossary

chips, usually not cooked until crisp
soji – A starter to a rice dish, made from durum wheat and sweetened with sugar and cardamon. Also served as a dessert.
starpree – Deadbolt
stoep – Veranda
supari – Areca palm seeds
surah – A chapter/section of the Quran
Takleef maaf – Apologies for the imposition
tasbeeh – Prayer beads
tawah – Griddle pan
tiffin – Circular lunchbox type tins fitted together in a vertical pile. Tiffins are important in India as the gravy of a dish is not mixed with the rice and salad until just before lunch.
To hoo kareh? – What are you doing?

tsotsi – South African slang for gangster or petty criminal
Übermensch – A person who seems superhuman (German)
ubuntu – Concept of human kindness or humanity in a collective sense
ustaad – Teacher
vehlin – Rolling pin
voor – Literally, forward in Afrikaans. Used colloquially to indicate brazenness.
wali – Religious mentor
wuss – Slang for weakling
Ya Allah – Oh, God; Oh, my God
Zuhr – Second Islamic prayer of the day, often performed in the hour before or after midday, depending on the position of the sun

Acknowledgements

Jeremy Boraine and Jonathan Ball Publishers for believing that this was a story worth telling and my editor Angela Briggs, who made my voice sharper and clearer. The super-competent and meticulous Aimee Carelse for managing everything and everyone. Karabo K. Kgoleng and Ronnie Kasrils for their generous comments. Holmes the Creative for bringing my childhood neighbourhood to life on the cover.

Writing is a deeply personal journey. In the case of a memoir, perhaps more so. This book is the product of many people who have held my hand through the writing.

I thank:

My dear friend Cas Boorany, who passed away a few days before the final manuscript was delivered. But for Cas'

Acknowledgements

patience and calm disposition over the past few years, huge parts of this memoir would still have been sitting in *Notes* on my cell phone. Cas put together for me a coherent 65 000-word first draft and gave it the look and feel of a serious writer's touch. It will always remain painful for me that he did not live to hold this book in his hands.

Professor Sumaya Laher, my childhood friend and an outstanding academic. She understood on so many levels why this book was important to me. Thank you for mentoring me through the creative and technical process and giving me access to your brilliant mind whenever I asked. There were times when my writing chugged along on your optimism alone. This book is as much yours as it is mine.

My friend Fathema Bemath, who has patiently shared with me her perspectives of life and love and whose compassion and kindness influenced the tone of so many of my stories. Being your friend makes me look at the world differently.

Shahana Theba, for giving me the privilege of being the younger sister. Sa'diyya Saloojee, for showing me what fearlessness looks like. Andy Appalsamy, Ameera Sarfudin, Aatika Deedat and Raasha Jina for patiently enduring almost every rant I have had. It must be exhausting being friends with me. Thank you. Reyhana A Satar for a Saturday night crash course in architecture and helping me to understand how politicised design and space are.

Ruby Patel and Dr Ian Opperman for showing me that, despite the ugliness, it is still a beautiful world.

My cousin Riaz Solker, who manages to centre me, ground me and sometimes gently remind me of my insignificance while simultaneously making me feel valued, appreciated and loved. It is a superpower.

The extraordinary Vally family. Thank you for trusting me with our stories and graciously allowing me to use our name. I hope that I have done a decent job, that you recognise us on these pages.

My parents, Ally and Julie Theba. Thank you for a lifetime of unconditional love. I have your support even when we all know that I am about to make a huge mistake. And thank you for the music.

My sons Mikaeel and Amaan, who have taught me how to eat humble pie graciously, call me out frequently and challenge me daily. I have learnt the most about myself from the two of you. I pray that the world is kind to you.

Finally, and most importantly, my husband Yusuf. Thank you for the laughter, the dance parties, the kitchen experiments and introducing this city person to Nature. Mostly, thank you for holding everything together when the world falls out from under us. After twenty years of partnering with my favourite person in the world, I cannot imagine having seen this project through without your love and support.

About the author

Razina Theba is a mother and an attorney. She lives in Johannesburg with her husband and sons.

www.ingramcontent.com/pod-product-compliance
Lightning Source LLC
Chambersburg PA
CBHW070840160426
43192CB00012B/2252